FOLLOW THE TREND

WHEN TO BUY AND WHEN TO SELL

by

M.G. BUCHOLTZ
B.Sc., MBA, M.Sc.

OTHER BOOKS BY M.G. BUCHOLTZ

FINANCIAL MARKETS

Stock Market Forecasting: The McWhirter Method De-Mystified
The Bull, The Bear and The Planets: Trading the Financial Markets Using Astrology
The Cosmic Clock: Timing the Financial Markets Using the Planets
The Lost Science: Esoteric Math and Astrology Techniques for the Market Trader
Financial Astrology Almanac 2023: Trading & Investing Using the Planets (11th Edition)
Financial Astrology Almanac 2022: Trading & Investing Using the Planets (10th Edition)
Financial Astrology Almanac 2021: Trading & Investing Using the Planets (19th Edition)
Financial Astrology Almanac 2020: Trading & Investing Using the Planets (8th Edition)
Financial Astrology Almanac 2019: Trading & Investing Using the Planets (7th Edition)
Financial Astrology Almanac 2018: Trading & Investing Using the Planets (6th Edition)
Financial Astrology Almanac 2017: Trading & Investing Using the Planets (5th Edition)
Financial Astrology Almanac 2016: Trading & Investing Using the Planets (4th Edition)
Financial Astrology Almanac 2015: Trading & Investing Using the Planets (3rd Edition)
Financial Astrology Almanac 2014: Trading & Investing Using the Planets (2nd Edition)
Financial Astrology Almanac 2013: Trading & Investing Using the Planets (1st Edition)

SCIENCE

The Recipe: Reviving the Lost Art of Home Distilling
Field to Flask: The Fundamentals of Small Batch Distilling (5th Edition)
Frozen Fury: Agricultural Crops and Hail Damage

POLITICS AND SOCIAL ISSUES

Thatcher versus Douglas - Subtitle: The CCF, the Liberals, and the Mossbank Debate of 1957

FOLLOW THE TREND

WHEN TO BUY AND WHEN TO SELL

by

M.G. BUCHOLTZ
B.Sc., MBA, M.Sc.

A Wood Dragon Book

FOLLOW THE TREND
WHEN TO BUY AND WHEN TO SELL

Cover design by: Callum Jagger/Hyperlight Artwork
Inside Design by: Christine Lee

First Edition

Published by:
Wood Dragon Books
Box 429, Mossbank, Saskatchewan, Canada S0H 3G0
http://www.wooddragonbooks.com

Contact the author:
Email: supercyclereport@gmail.com
Website: www.investingsuccess.ca

ISBN: 978-1-990863-18-9 (eBook)
ISBN: 978-1-990863-17-2 (paperback)

DEDICATION

To Ron, Ted, and Sheldon

CONTENTS

INTRODUCTION

In the aftermath of the tragic terrorist events of September 11, 2001, I started to think about the future. The world had just taken a staggering lurch in an unexpected direction. I wondered what this new global direction would hold in store for me.

I had just finished my MBA degree studies and was still working in the steel industry. I felt unchallenged. The management style of the company I was working for was deeply rooted in the time and motion, carrot-and-stick mantra of the 1950s. I was not happy.

I had a burning desire to start applying the knowledge I had gained from my MBA studies. One day, my wife and I found ourselves enmeshed in a deep conversation. In light of the 9-11 terrorist attack, we agreed that life could be short. She asked me point blank, "If you could do anything you wanted, work anywhere you wanted, follow your passion, what would you do?" My answer was equally pointed, "I would become a stockbroker."

An unusual answer for a person with no sales background. An unusual answer for a person with no family history of stock market investing. But I had a deep, almost unsatiable interest in the financial markets. In hindsight, I realize now that my aggressive, Type A personality viewed the markets as something to be conquered; something to be mastered; a mountain to be climbed.

I made arrangements to meet with my Investment Advisor who had recently left Merrill Lynch to join a small, independent firm called Union Securities. We talked about opportunities in the investment business and he agreed to set up a meeting with his Branch Manager. When I eventually met with the Branch Manager, it was made clear to me that if I were to join the investment industry the road ahead would be filled with challenges and hard work. There was no guarantee I would enjoy myself. There was certainly no guarantee of success. But if I was willing to take the chance, an opportunity could be made available. I immediately started studying the textbooks for the requisite exams: the Canadian Securities Course, the Ethics and Conduct Course, the Options Licensing Course, and the Futures Licensing Course. With relative ease, I passed these requisite exams one after another.

In April of 2002, it was a glorious day when I finally left my job in the steel industry. I bade farewell to the carrot-and-stick management approach, the lack of intellectual challenge, and the toxic relationships with the labor unions. I was now on my way to becoming a licensed Investment Advisor.

As I settled into my new role, my Branch Manager wasted little time making it clear to me that following the trend of a stock, a commodity future, or an equity index was the key to success. He stressed that the trend could be gleaned from applying technical indicators to daily and weekly charts. He cautioned that *not* paying attention to the trend would be stressful for both me and my clients.

He was right. When the markets were rising, clients never called. When the markets were falling, they called—a lot. But no matter which way the markets were moving, who I did receive phone calls from were mutual fund sales representatives. Everybody's fund was the best one to buy. Every fund's manager was the superstar to follow. Every fund had a unique investment approach. Value, growth, enterprise value ratios; I heard it all. I soon figured out that the investment industry was structured around precepts like *Modern Portfolio Theory*, and the *Frontier Efficiency Curve*. Selling clients on the notion of investing for the long term was the name of the mutual fund game. My Branch Manager's strategy of following the trend to time the market was not condoned by the sales reps whose mutual funds dominated the investment landscape. Gradually, the phone calls diminished. I was a rebel. Mutual fund sales reps learned not to waste their time calling me.

In 2004, I enrolled in the hallowed Chartered Financial Analyst (CFA) program. My hunger for knowledge was immense. I wanted to figure out how the financial industry really worked. I wanted to get right to the heart of it. I knew that fund managers did not just sit on a portfolio of stocks. Behind the scenes, they were buying and selling. How did they decide when to buy and when to sell? As I worked diligently to identify new clients and bring in accounts, I devoted evenings and weekends to studying CFA textbooks. But as I learned about dividend discount models and bootstrapping yield curves, the words of my Branch Manager resonated in my head, "Follow the trend. Follow the trend."

As I continued to steep myself in CFA material, I also continued to gather more information on chart technical indicators that could help me identify the trend. I found that indicators like RSI and MAC-D were commonly used, but strategies for properly using these indicators were not well defined. There was only one other advisor in the office, a seasoned veteran commodity broker, who was able to shed any light on these indicators. With his assistance, I found myself better understanding some of these indicators. "Follow the trend. Follow the trend." This soon became my mantra.

In early 2006, something unexpected happened. I hit a mental roadblock. One of the textbooks I was using to study for CFA Level 2 stated that technical chart analysis *did not* work. In fact, the textbook almost made a mockery of those who used chart analysis. I abruptly lost interest in the CFA program. The contrarian streak in me started wondering if the CFA program perhaps felt threatened by technical chart analysis. There had to be more to technical chart analysis than I realized. Why else would the CFA program so pointedly refute technical analysis? As I divorced myself from my CFA studies, I decided to focus even more intently on stock charts and technical indicators. I decided to focus on individual stocks. I stopped taking calls from mutual fund peddlers altogether. "Follow the trend. Follow the trend."

By mid-2006, I found myself focusing on energy and mining stocks. With my engineering degree, I was able to understand structural geology, mineral formations, and the basics of oil and gas deposits. I could explain the salient details of resource companies to clients. I was able to apply chart trend indicators to resource stocks. I was learning new things. My voracious appetite for learning was being sated.

One financial product that was hugely popular in the resource sector in 2006 was the income trust structure. To reduce corporate taxes, companies would pay out a generous pre-tax dividend to shareholders. To compensate for this payout and yet maintain working capital for additional exploration and development, resource companies would issue more and more share units as well as debentures with attractive coupon yields. As an Investment Advisor, I was providing clients with a money-making investment product. I was also getting rewarded with some very comfortable sales commissions. What could go wrong?

The answer to this question rudely knocked on the door on Halloween 2006. Canadian federal finance minister Jim Flaherty abruptly passed legislation that killed the income trust structure. He was apparently alarmed at the declining stream of tax revenues accruing to the Canadian government. Instead of prohibiting the formation of new income trusts, he killed the entire field. The value of income trust share units in client portfolios slumped. The golden goose was dead. Almost overnight, my energy level deflated. As I patiently waited for senior management at Union Securities to identify new investment products to provide to clients, I started having dark thoughts. Had my Investment Advisor experience run its course? Was it time to move on to new challenges? I was fascinated with the resource sector. Could I parlay my investment industry knowledge into a new opportunity in the mining industry?

A few months later, in early 2007, my questions were answered. An opportunity to join the management team at a Saskatchewan-based junior uranium exploration company materialized. I jumped at the chance to become their V.P. of Investor Relations. In 2008, opportunity again beckoned. The CEO of the company found himself in deep hot water with Canadian securities regulators. Apparently they had been watching his shady activity for several years. At the behest of the Ontario Securities Commission, the Board of Directors terminated him. The Board asked me to step in to fill the CEO role. I took immediate steps to begin cleaning up the company's balance sheet. Over the next eight years, I steered this junior company in an entirely new direction; away from uranium exploration in northern Saskatchewan and into rare earth exploration in New Mexico, USA.

Staking claims, examining rock formations, and determining drill locations in the Gallinas Mountains of New Mexico kept me more than busy, but I still carved out time to continue learning more about technical chart analysis. I poured over stock and commodity charts, I read monthly magazines on technical analysis, and I laid hands on whatever material I could find related to W.D. Gann.

My interest in Gann had come about because of my involvement with Freemasonry. One evening while doing some reading in the local Grand Lodge Masonic library, I learned that W.D. Gann had been a Mason.

I soon found myself seeking out material on chart patterns and sacred geometry. Was there a connection to the stock market? What did Gann know? Were sacred geometry and patterns related to the price trend of stocks and indices?

Early 2012 would answer these questions in a resounding way. On a return trip to Canada, I was sitting in a hotel room in a small town somewhere in Wyoming. I was checking what the markets had done that day and doing research into new resource stocks. While searching for information on W.D. Gann, I stumbled upon an ad for an upcoming astrology conference in New Orleans, Louisiana. I am not sure what piqued my interest in this ad; I had not even considered using astrology as a tool to discern the ups and downs of markets. Perhaps my exposure to Freemasonry with its veiled astrology references made me take a second look at this advertisement. With a couple clicks of the mouse, I landed on the website for the UAC 2012 Astrology Conference. The conference agenda showed there would be a series of plenary sessions related to financial astrology. My mind began to reel. Sacred geometry, patterns, planets, W.D. Gann. Was it all related? "Follow the trend. Follow the trend."

I registered for the conference, reasoning that whether I enjoyed the conference or not, my wife and I would enjoy some quality time every evening at the Spotted Cat music bar on Frenchman Street in New Orleans' Faubourg Marigny neighborhood. As I sat through the various conference sessions, I became convinced that I had found the missing link. I learned about cyclical patterns on price charts. I learned about cosmic events such as planetary retrograde, declination, and Moon phases. I learned that W.D. Gann had used astrology to make buying and selling decisions. I learned about Louise McWhirter and her 18.6-year economic cycle. I learned that the time series price data for a stock, commodity, or index is not random; the ups and downs of a chart are made up of overlapping, interwoven cycles. Taken together, all of these cosmic factors and cycles helped to define the price trend.

I left the New Orleans conference feeling elated; I was walking on air. I had just found the missing link. The markets were not about buying and holding, efficiency hypotheses, or dividend discount models. The markets were about the trend. The trend was influenced by cycles and patterns in the cosmos; cycles and patterns of planetary movement that affected the psyche of people and made them buy or sell. I needed to learn more.

On trips to London, UK to promote the junior mining company, I would take time to explore bookstores around the Charring Cross area in search of books about cycles, Gann, and astrology. I even combed my way through the stacks at the British Library. In 2013, I wrote two books to codify the knowledge I had amassed: *The Bull, Bear and Planets* and *The Lost Science*. I also started writing a bi-weekly newsletter called the *Astrology Letter*.

I did not stop at these two books. Since 2013, I have authored 15 books on the subject of financial astrology. In addition to newsletter writing and book publishing, I also make myself available to people seeking a personalized coaching session to learn more about the connection between the trend, cycles, and events in the cosmos. But I have noticed there is a problem. People who have contacted me for coaching do not grasp what the trend is. They make investment decisions based on hearsay, television personalities, meme stocks in the news, internet Reddit opinion, and lately, the Robin Hood network. Trying to explain the concept of the trend on a telephone call or a Zoom chat has proven difficult. That is why I decided to write this book.

There are many market data platforms available to individual traders and investors; Interactive Brokers, TD Ameritrade, Scotia-iTrade, to name a few. Each platform comes pre-programmed with various technical chart indicators to help a person discern price movements. But what do these indicators mean? How should they be interpreted? How should their input parameters be set? How do they indicate a trend change? Do they even work?

This book is designed to be a reference resource to help readers better understand the formulas and the mathematics behind the various chart indicators that can be used to discern price trends. This book starts with a look at the information revealed by different types of price bars on charts. This leads to a look at moving averages as a trend change indicator. The book then goes deeper to explore a wide range of oscillator type indicators. As traders and investors create charts on their computer screens, this book can be used as a guide to apply and configure trend indicators to the charts.

One thing this book will *not* do is discuss planets and astrology. The focus of this book will strictly be on interpreting the changes of price trend and using technical chart indicators. I can tell you, however, that many of the swing highs and lows that define changes to the trend do bear a strong correlation to planetary events. For anyone seeking to eventually make that connection, I suggest obtaining my annual *Financial Astrology Almanac* and reading it in conjunction with this book.

As I crafted this manuscript, I reflected on the past 21 years, thinking about the discussion in 2001 when my wife asked me what I would do if I could do anything I wanted. I kept thinking about all that has transpired over the past two decades. Had I not been offered a chance to join the investment industry; had my Branch Manager not been a strict adherent of trend following; had I not become a Freemason; had I not attended the astrology conference in New Orleans; had I not realized that W.D. Gann had been both a Mason and an astrologer, and had my junior company promotion efforts not led me to the British Library and Charring Cross bookstores, I would not be penning this book. Everything happens for a reason. Maybe one day I will come to understand the reason; why me, why all this knowledge, why here, why now?

CHAPTER 1
CHARTING

Charting the Price Data

The first step in following the trend and deciding when to buy and sell is to create a visual representation of the price data for the stock, ETF, or commodity futures contract a trader is interested in. The visual representation is called a price chart. A price chart comprises time on the horizontal axis and price on the vertical axis. The increments of time for the horizontal axis afford numerous possibilities. For example, a *price chart* can display price action for increments of 5 minutes, 10 minutes, 30 minutes, 60 minutes, 4 hours, one day, one week, one month and so on.

Once the time increment has been decided on, the software provided as part of a brokerage account platform will generate a price chart. The trader or investor can then select from a variety of ways to display the price data on the chart.

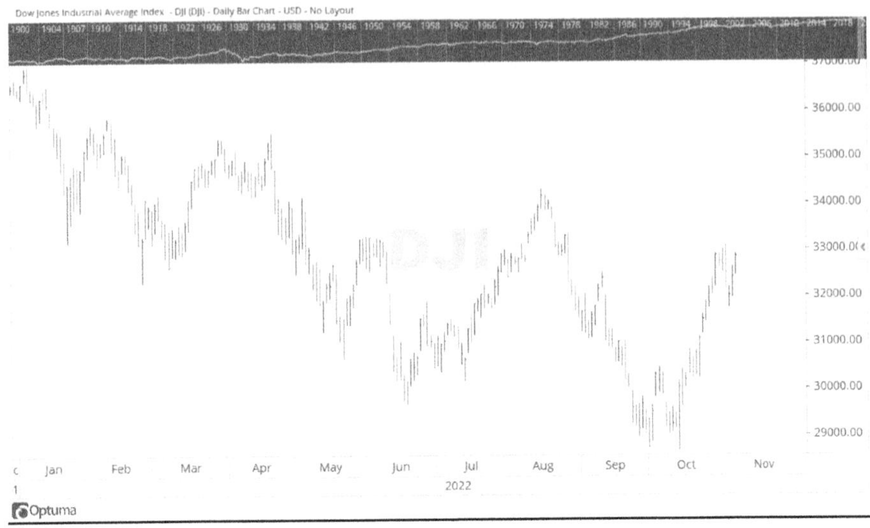

Figure 1-1

Dow Jones Industrial Average in bar chart format

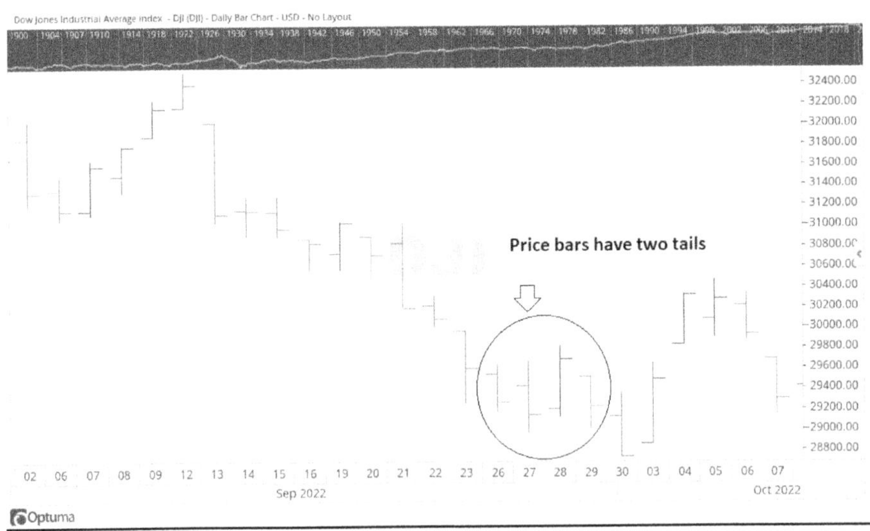

Figure 1-2

Dow Jones Industrial Average bar chart bars

Bar Chart

The standard style setting on a typical trading software platform is the *bar chart*. Each bar on the price chart will record the data for the time increment stipulated: 5 minutes, 10 minutes, 30 minutes, 60 minutes, 4 hours, daily, weekly, monthly, and so on. Figure 1-1 illustrates daily price action on the Dow Jones Industrial Average in bar chart format. Each bar (which resembles a line) is comprised of the open, high, low, and closing price. The high price for the bar is the top of the bar; the low price is the bottom of the bar.

The bars on a bar chart will be colored. Default settings are usually red and blue. Red signifies a bar on which the closing price is less than the opening price. Blue signifies a bar on which the closing price is higher than the opening price. Each bar will have two small tails, as illustrated in Figure 1-2. The tail on the left side of a bar indicates the opening price for the time frame represented by the bar; the tail on the right side indicates the closing price.

Candlestick Chart

Another style configuration is the *candlestick chart*. The candlesticks on a chart are presented in black and white (hollow) format as illustrated in Figure 1-3. The daily candlesticks circled are from the same dates as the daily bars that are circled in Figure 1-2.

There are no tails on the left and right side of a candlestick. The shading of the candlesticks tells the price story. A hollow body on a candlestick indicates a closing price higher than that of the opening price. A solid black body on a candlestick indicates a closing price below that of the opening price.

In Figure 1-2, the price bars for September 26 and 27 had the closing price less than the opening price. In Figure 1-3, the candlesticks for September

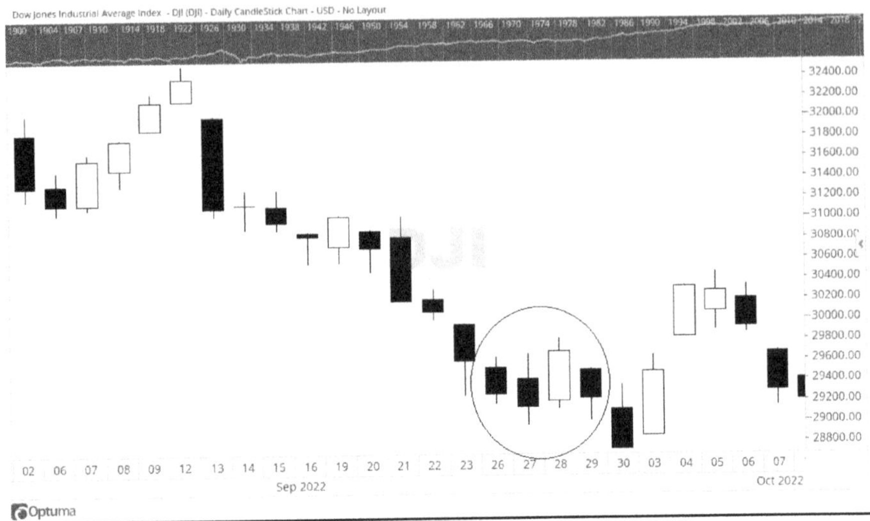

Figure 1-3

Dow Jones Industrial Average with candlesticks

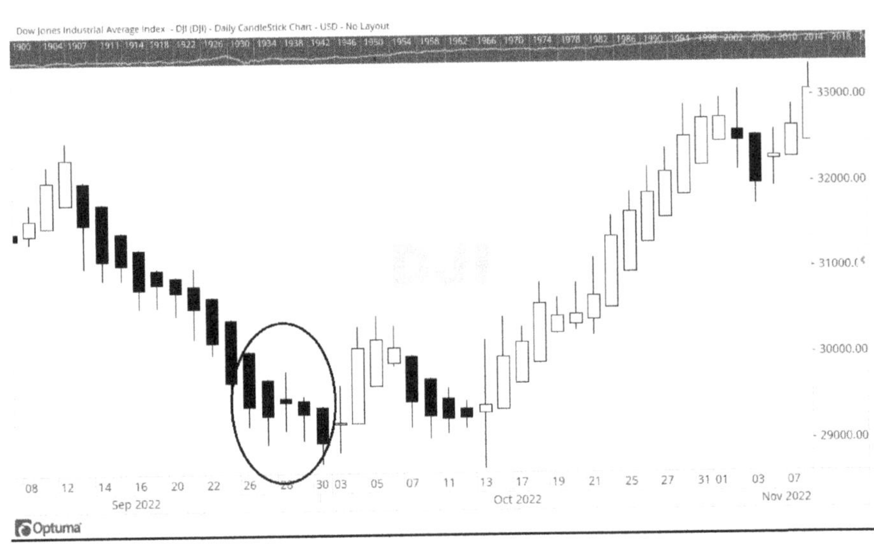

Figure 1-4

Dow Jones Industrial Average with Heiken-Ashi bars

26 and 27 appear as solid black, indicating that the closing price was less than the opening price. In Figure 1-2, the price bar for September 28 had the closing price greater than the opening price. In Figure 1-3, the candlestick for September 28 appears as hollow thus indicating a closing price above the opening price. In a solid black candlestick, the opening price is identified by the top of the rectangular shaped candlestick; the closing price is denoted by the bottom of the rectangular shaped candlestick. With a hollow bar, the opposite holds true. The opening price is identified by the bottom of the rectangular shaped candlestick; the closing price is denoted by the top of the rectangular shaped candlestick.

Each candlestick will have vertical tails projecting above and below it. These tails indicate the price high and price low recorded during the time period covered by the candlestick. These tails provide insight into the emotions of buyers and sellers. A candlestick consisting of a small rectangular body and a large tail (or tails) projecting from it suggests that during the period of time covered by the candlestick, buyers and sellers were uncertain about the price trend. Traders bid prices up significantly during the timeframe covered by the candlestick, but then also engaged in substantial selling. Uncertainty dominated the emotions of traders. The appearance of a sequence of consecutive candlesticks also provide insight into the sentiment of traders. Solid black candlesticks followed by a succession of hollow candlesticks suggest that traders and investors were starting to feel more bullish. Hollow candlesticks followed by a series of black candlesticks suggest the onset of bearish, negative sentiments.

Candlestick charts trace their history back to 1700's Japan. Munehisa Homma, a Japanese rice trader at the Dojima rice market in Osaka, began charting the daily price figures he recorded from observing rice traders conduct rice sales. He plotted candlestick bars on a paper chart where each candlestick expressed the open, close, high and low price he had observed that day. It was Homma who is credited with the idea that price candlesticks offer insight into the emotions of traders.

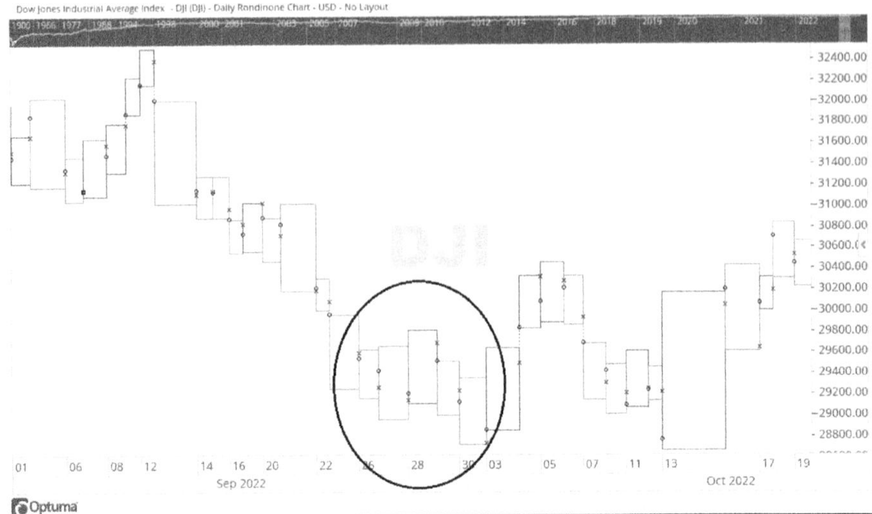

Figure 1-5

Dow Jones Industrial Average with Rondinone bars

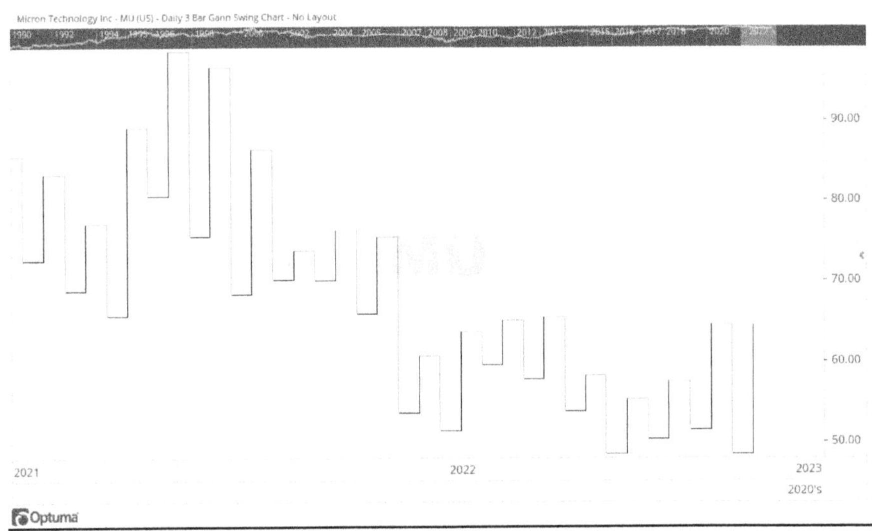

Figure 1-6

Micron Technology (MU) in Gann Swing Chart format

Munehisa Homma went on to refine his candlesticks. The outcome of his refinement efforts is called *Heiken-Ashi candlesticks*. Each Heiken-Ashi candlestick is designed to better reflect changes in price trend.

The opening price of a given Heiken Ashi candlestick is taken as the average of the previous candlestick's high and low price. The closing price of a given candlestick is calculated as the average of high, low, open, and close. The following equations illustrate further:

Open = ½ [open of previous candlestick + close of previous candlestick]
Close = ¼ [high + low+open+close]
High = max [high, open, close]
Low = min [low, open, close].

Figure 1-4 shows a circle around the same candlesticks as in Figure 1-3. The solid appearance of these candlesticks indicates the sellers were prevailing and emotion was negative. In fact, the trend was negative.

Rondinone Chart

The software provided as part of a brokerage account is likely to contain a variety of charting methods. Perhaps this makes the user feel more empowered knowing that multiple charting options are available.

Another chart configuration that might be encountered on various software platforms is the Rondinone chart. This format is named after Joe Rondinone who is said to have been one of the last people to have been personally tutored by W.D. Gann.

Figure 1-5 shows a circle around some candlestick bars. A closer look at Figure 1-5 shows that the vertical sides of each bar contain a small 'x' and/or a small 'o'. On the left side of a bar, the 'o' denotes the opening price. On the right side of a bar, the 'x' denotes the closing price. Further study of Figure 1-5 shows the bars are of varying widths. One of the formulas

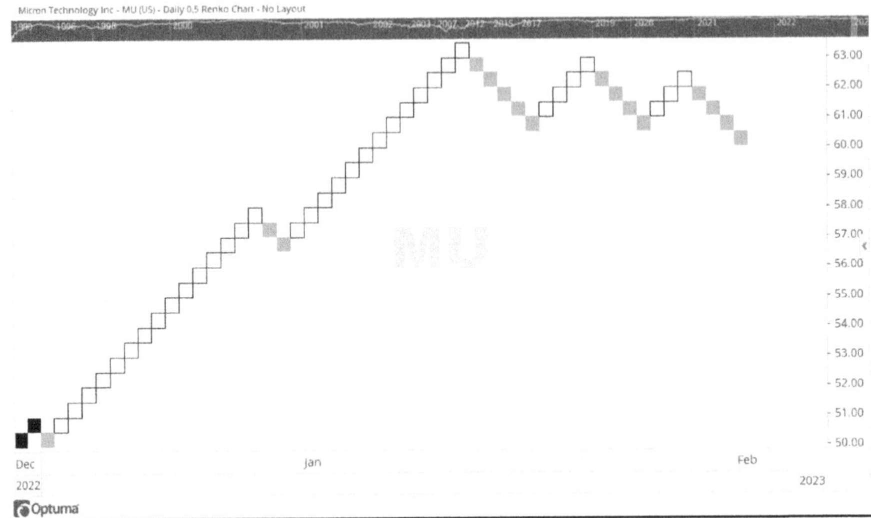

Figure 1-7

Micron Technology (MU) in Renko chart format

that Rondinone used for determining bar width was: (bar high minus bar low) x 0.382. The 0.382 figure is clearly a reference to Fibonacci and the Golden Mean. In researching Rondinone, the rationale for altering bar width could not be clarified. Yet, software platforms make it a point to provide users with the ability to configure a chart using Rondinone bars. If I cannot be provided with an explanation as to why a price bar is configured the way it is, then I will not use that charting method.

Gann Swing, Kagi, Point & Figure, Renko, and more...

The list of chart presentation types that are programmed into software platforms goes well beyond what has been discussed in this chapter. I make it a point to ignore the more unusual chart types. As I see it, all that is needed to identify the trend and decide on buying and selling is a chart that shows open, high, low, and closing prices. By proving myriad chart types, perhaps software providers are trying to make users feel they have obtained value for money spent.

For example, Figure 1-6 illustrates the daily price action on semiconductor chip maker Micron Technology in *Gann Swing* format. The lines on the chart are shaded darker and lighter. The darker-shaded lines depict spans of time when price was moving higher. Lighter-shaded lines depict spans of time when price was moving lower. The chart settings are configured such that it would take three days of falling prices to create a lighter-shaded line. At the right side of the chart, notice that the vertical line is darker-shaded. At this time of writing in early February 2023, price of Micron shares has not exhibited three consecutive days of lower closing prices. An interesting observation for sure, but this style of chart offers no practical way for a trader or investor to identify a precise buy or sell point.

As another example, Figure 1-7 illustrates price action of Micron Technology in *Renko* chart format. The chart settings are such that a new hollow diamond-shaped box on the chart will form each time closing price advances 50 cents or more from the previous day. A new dark-colored diamond will form each time closing price declines 50 cents or more from the previous day. All very interesting observations for sure, but this style of chart offers no practical way for a trader or investor to identify a precise buy or sell point.

18

CHAPTER 2
THE TREND ACCORDING TO GANN

The Trend

The dictionary definition of *trend* is: *a general direction in which something is developing or changing.*

In the context of the financial markets, the trend is the general direction in which price is traveling. A strategy of following the trend means that traders and investors will closely follow price charts; price on the vertical axis and time on the horizontal axis. They will be focused on times when the price of a stock, commodity, or index ETF stops traveling in one general direction and starts moving in the opposite direction. Changes in trend demand action on the part of the trader or investor. For a stock, commodity, or ETF that has been exhibiting declining price action, a change of trend will translate into a buying opportunity. For a stock, commodity, or ETF that has been exhibiting rising price action, a change in trend will likely lead to a selling decision. A change of trend could also present an opportunity for a call option or put option strategy. A change in trend could also just mean that a stop-loss order gets re-adjusted.

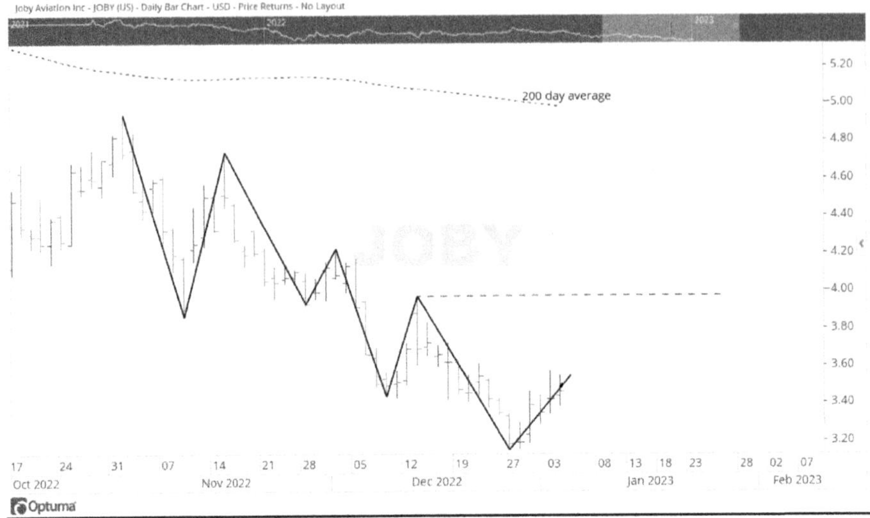

Figure 2-1

Joby Aviation (JOBY) showing swings

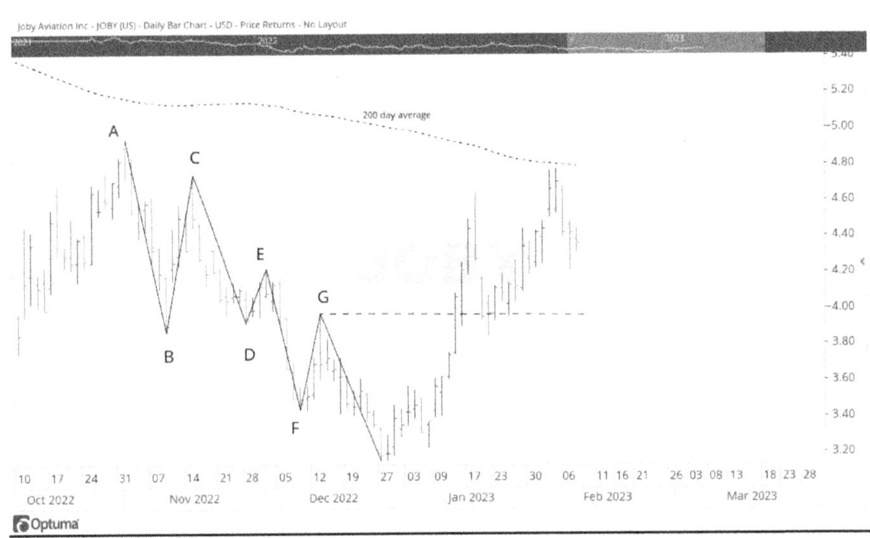

Figure 2-2

Joby Aviation (JOBY) showing swings

Gann's Trend Rules

While compiling this manuscript, I discovered a book written by trader Robert Krausz. I further discovered that Krausz had written the book to codify some of Gann's learning course material. In 1955, Joe Rondinone was one of the last people to be tutored by W.D. Gann. Several decades later, Mr. Rondinone sold his Gann learning material to Robert Krausz on the proviso that Krausz use the material and go on to share it with others. Mr. Krausz did exactly that. The book manuscript he was working on at the time of his death in 2002 was subsequently published in 2005 by Mr. Krausz's associates.

According to Krausz, Gann focused on the 'swing point' and the 'trend'. Gann defined the swing point as the price bar where the *direction of travel* changes. Figure 2-1 illustrates daily price action on Joby Aviation. This company is developing a lithium-ion battery powered vertical take-off and landing aircraft that is capable of transporting up to four passengers.

In Figure 2-1, tops and bottoms of price bars have been joined with solid black lines. Each time one of these line segments changes from being in an upslope to being in a downslope, the swing is said to have changed.

The Prior Peak Rule

One rule that Gann developed concerning swings is to watch for times when the swing changes and goes on to surpass a recent peak point. This, he called the Prior Peak rule. In Figure 2-2, swing points have been labeled as A, B, C, D, E F, and G. A trader seeking to take a long position in JOBY would buy if, and only if, the price of the stock surpassed the prior peak. Swing point C failed to surpass point A. Swing point E failed to surpass point C. Swing point G failed to surpass point E. However, a buy signal was created when price surpassed point G ($3.96 per share).

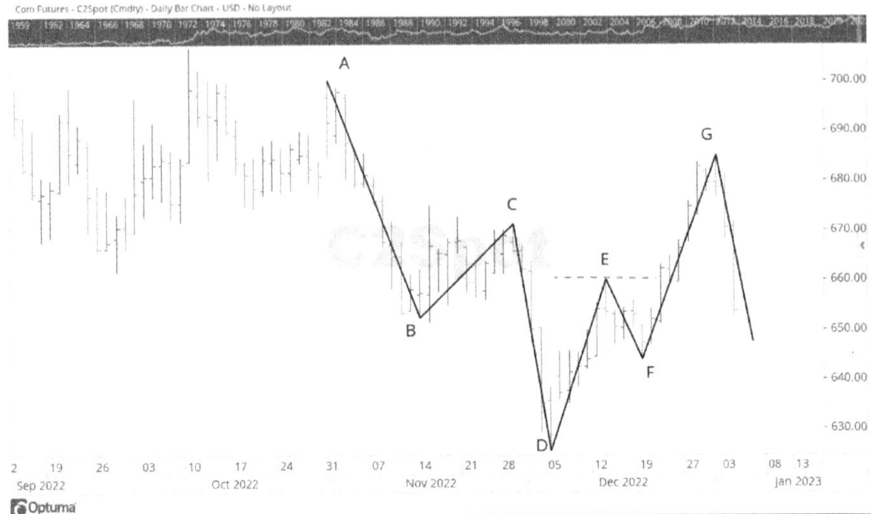

Figure 2-3

Corn futures (daily) showing swings

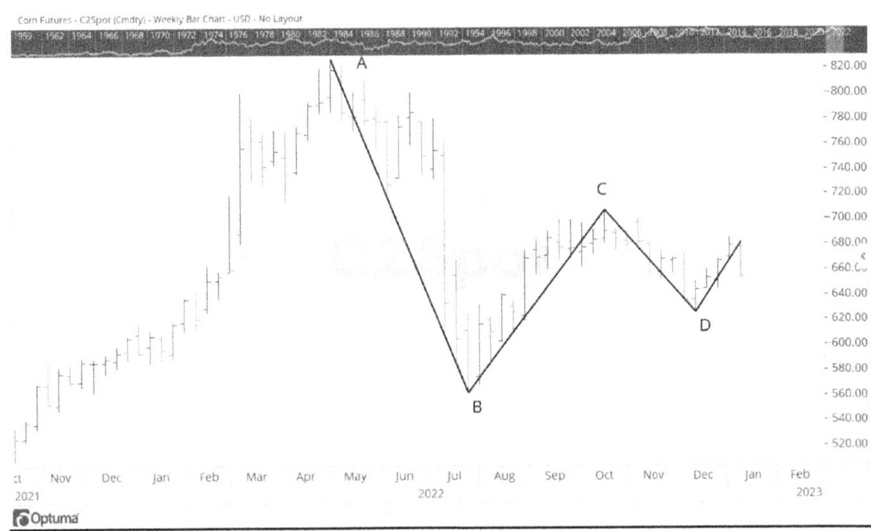

Figure 2-4

Corn futures (weekly) showing swings

Figure 2-3 illustrates a continuous front month daily price chart for Corn futures. Seven swing points, labeled A through G, have been identified on the chart. A trader seeking to take a long position in Corn futures would have bought as price surpassed Point E at $6.60. From this entry point, price moved 25 cents higher (that is a $1250 move on a contract of Corn) before hitting Point G where the swing changed.

Commodity futures are notoriously more volatile than most stocks. To maintain perspective, W.D. Gann advised to examine a weekly chart. Figure 2-4 illustrates the Corn futures price action in weekly chart format.

The weekly corn chart in Figure 2-4 has been overlaid with swing points labeled A, B, C, and D. This longer-time horizon chart tells a slightly different tale. In this chart, Point C failed to surpass Point A. A trader seeking to buy Corn futures using the Gann Prior Peak method would do so if price moves above Point C ($6.90). A trader using the prior swing method on a daily chart as shown in Figure 2-2 would therefore adopt a cautious mindset, knowing that a long position had been taken in the context of a weekly chart that still had not offered a buy signal.

A trader seeking to take short positions, knowing that the trend on Corn futures is bearish, would look for price bars that break below a prior valley. Referring back to Figure 2-3, after Point C, a short position would have been initiated as price moved beneath Point B. A short position would be in order if price violates Point F ($6.44).

The Two Bar Swing Change Rule

W.D. Gann further focused on price behavior around swing points. One rule he defined is called the Two Bar Swing Change Rule. Gann advised that a trader should wait until two consecutive price bars after the swing point provided confirmation that the trend had changed. In the case of a swing point that is a price low (*a valley*), a trader will require two consecutive price bars each exhibiting a higher high. In the case of a swing

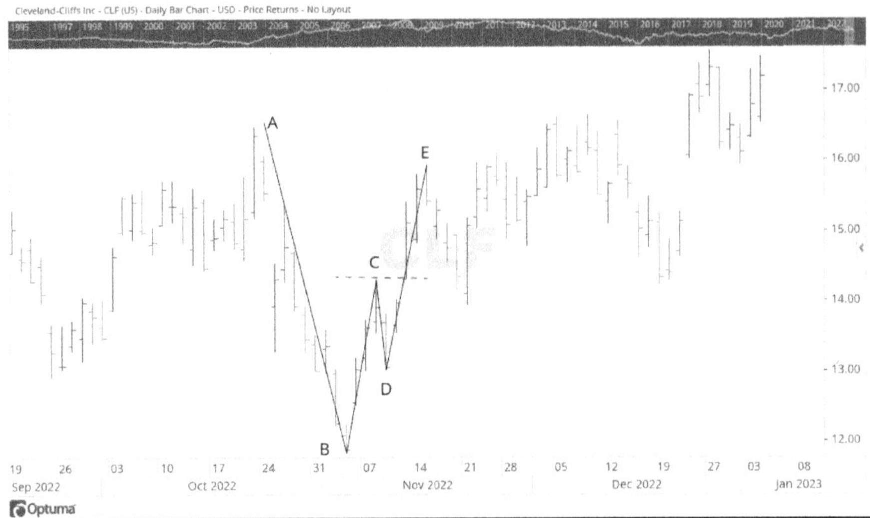

Figure 2-5

NYSE:CLF showing swings

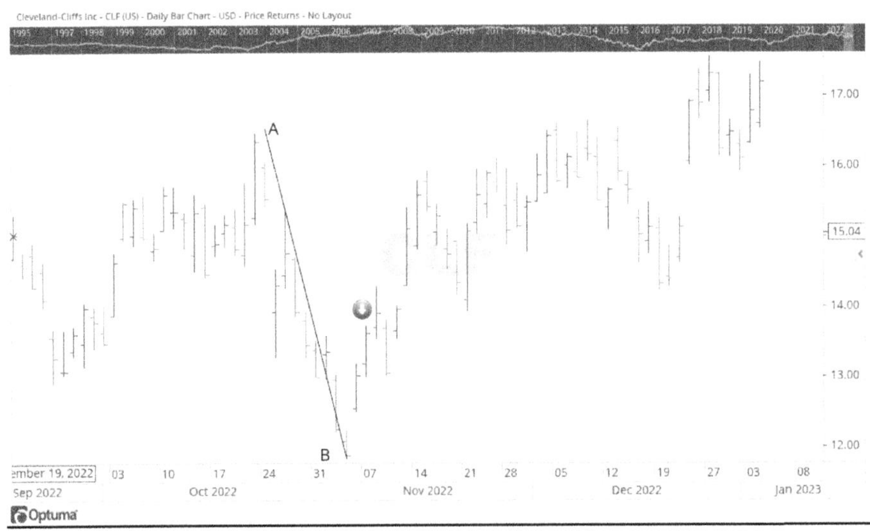

Figure 2-6

NYSE:CLF showing swings

point that is a price high (a peak), a trader will require two consecutive price bars each exhibiting a lower low.

Figures 2-5 and 2-6 compare the Prior Peak Rule and the Two Bar Swing Change Rule in the context of daily price action on steelmaker Cleveland Cliffs (CLF).

In Figure 2-5, a trader using the Prior Peak Rule and seeking to take a long position would have bought as price moved above swing point C ($14.32). At Point E, price hit $15.39. On a suitable number of shares, this modest price gain would have yielded an acceptable profit for the three days it took for price to hit Point E.

Figure 2-6 illustrates the Two Bar Swing Change Rule. Point B was a price low, valley swing point. The two price bars that immediately followed Point B, each had a higher high. The arrow in Figure 2-6 shows where a trader would have taken a long position coming into the market close. The very next price bar turned in yet another higher high; the trader would no doubt be feeling satisfied. But the next price bar moved lower, triggering stop losses and bringing the trade strategy into question. Price then recovered and moved higher for the next several bars. By following the Two Bar Swing Change rule, the trader would have entered the trade at around $13.60, which is better than the $14.32 in Figure 2-4. However, the volatility *might* have caused the trader to panic and exit the trade. If a stop loss was being used, it may well have been triggered. Gann's Two Bar rule may have worked exceedingly well for him in 1955. But, today's volatile markets are far different from those of 1955.

The Hi-Lo Indicator Rule

Another swing rule that W.D. Gann illuminated in his course material involves the creation of a 3-day simple moving average using the low (or high) price data from the previous three price bars. My preference is to use the high points of price bars to calculate the 3-day average at a valley (swing

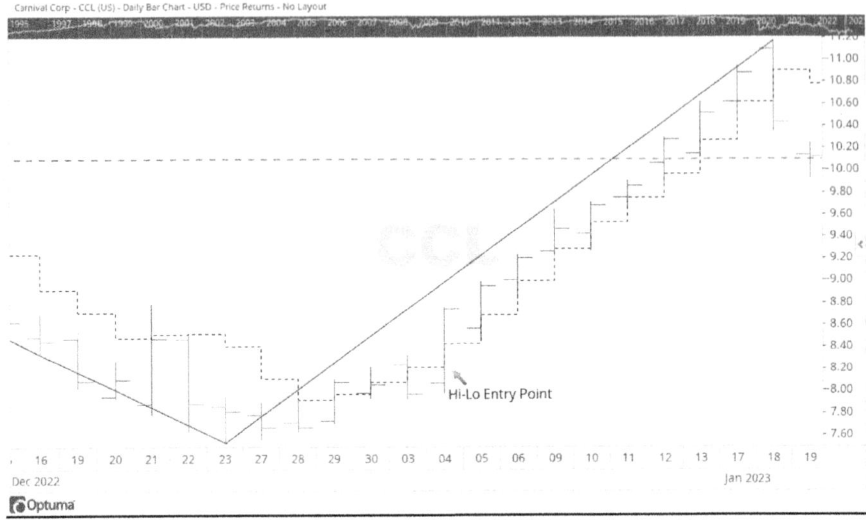

Figure 2-7

NYSE:CCL and the Hi-Lo indicator

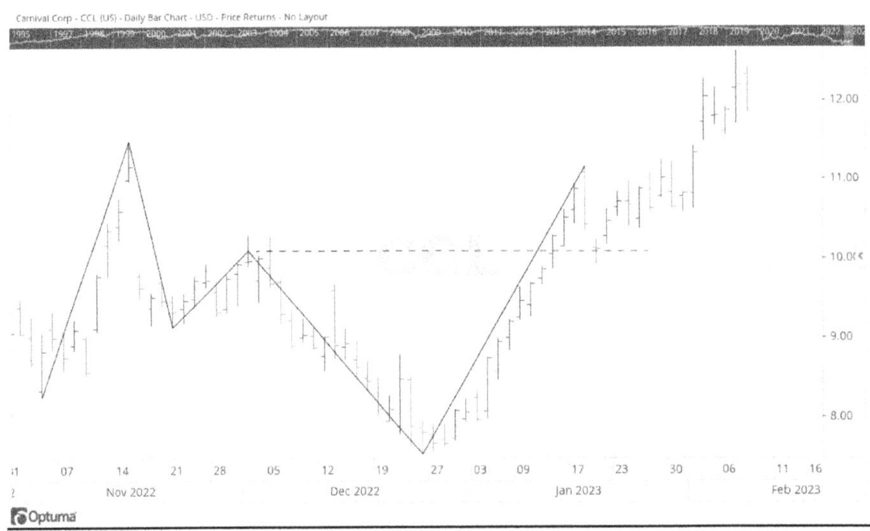

Figure 2-8

NYSE:CCL and the Hi-Lo indicator

low) and the low points of price bars to calculate the 3-day average at a swing high. Gann advised that once the swing point had been made, a trader should look for a subsequent price bar having a closing price above the bar that defined the valley (low). He likewise advised looking for a subsequent price bar having a closing price below the bar that defined the peak (high).

Consider the case of cruise line operator Carnival Corp (NYSE: CCL). A swing low point appeared on December 23, 2022. The step pattern overlaid on the chart in Figure 2-7 is the 3-day average, or what Gann called the Hi-Lo indicator.

At the date of the swing low, the 3-day moving average based on price highs was at $8.41. Following the swing bar, Gann's strategy was to buy on the bar that exhibited a closing price above the average that existed at the swing bar. It would not be until January 4, 2023 that this opportunity presented itself..

Figure 2-8 compares this Hi-Lo approach to the Prior Peak rule. Using the Prior Peak rule, a trader would have not entered a long trade until mid-January 2023. The entry price would have been just over the $10 level. Therefore, as a trader or investor, you will have to decide whether the Gann Prior Peak rule, Two Bar rule, or Hi-Lo rule suits your risk tolerance.

Figure 2-9 illustrates the use of the Two Bar swing rule. Following the valley low point, it would not be until bars 3 and 4 that this rule could have been applied. A trader would have entered the long position going into the market close at bar 4. The next day would have provided anxious moments as price retreated. But the next day, price moved smartly higher.

Each of these Gann rules would have provided different entry points for a trader seeking to take a long position in Carnival Corp shares. The choice of rule is a function of how much risk the trader is prepared to take. My personal preference is the Prior Peak Rule. What follows in this chapter

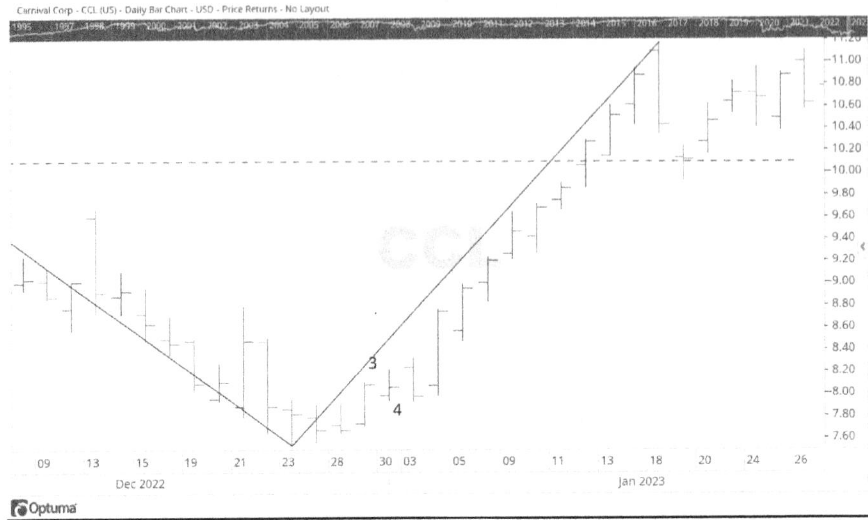

Figure 2-9

NYSE:CCL and the Two Bar Swing rule

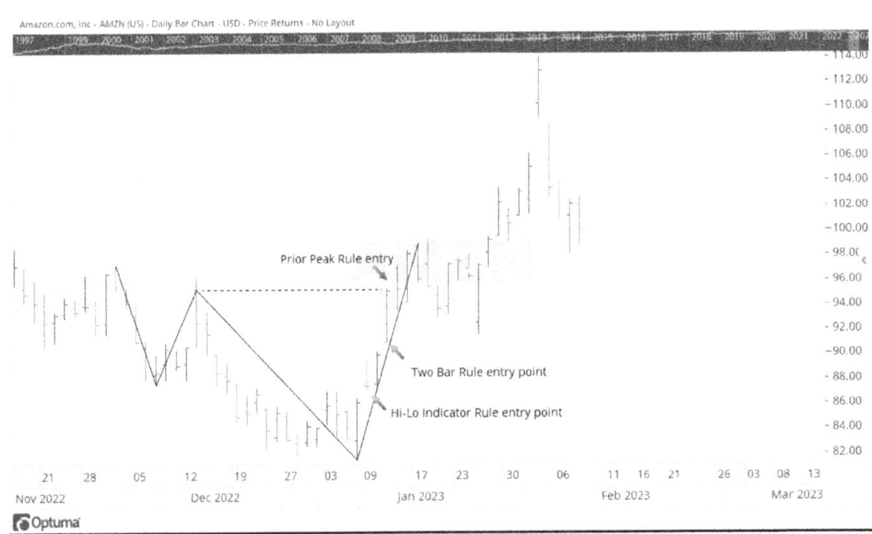

Figure 2-10

Amazon (AMZN) entry points

are a series of examples to more thoroughly indicate the application of this rule.

Figure 2-10 illustrates daily price action on Amazon (Nasdaq:AMZN) from late November 2022 into February 2023. The entry points for the Prior Peak rule, the Two Bar Swing rule, and the Hi-Lo Indicator rule are shown on the chart.

Figure 2-11 illustrates daily price action on Alphabet (Nasdaq:GOOG) from late November 2022 into February 2023. The entry points for the Prior Peak rule, the Two Bar Swing rule, and the Hi-Lo Indicator rule are shown on the chart.

Figure 2-12 illustrates daily price action on Livent (NYSE: LTHM) from December 2022 into February 2023. The entry points for the Prior Peak rule, the Two Bar Swing rule, and the Hi-Lo Indicator rule are shown on the chart. If you have purchased a re-chargeable device equipped with a lithium-ion battery lately, chances are the lithium in the battery was refined by Livent.

Figure 2-13 illustrates daily price action on ON Semiconductor (Nasdaq: ON) from late November 2022 into February 2023. The entry points for the Prior Peak rule, the Two Bar Swing rule, and the Hi-Lo Indicator rule are shown on the chart. Cloud computing, Internet of Things, automotive sensors and much more define what this company does.

Figure 2-14 illustrates daily price action on General Motors (NYSE: GM) from late November 2022 into February 2023. The entry points for the Prior Peak rule, the Two Bar Swing rule, and the Hi-Lo Indicator rule are shown on the chart. So far in 2023, General Motors has taken further steps to solidify its reputation as a vertically integrated automotive maker. It has inked a deal with a lithium mining project and is in advanced discussion over a nickel mining project. The nickel and lithium will be used to create its own line of EV car and light truck batteries.

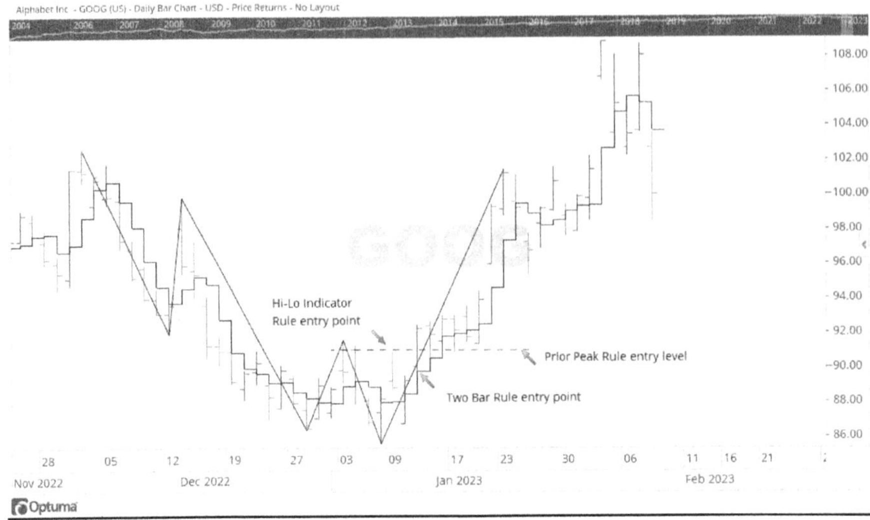

Figure 2-11

Alphabet (GOOG) entry points

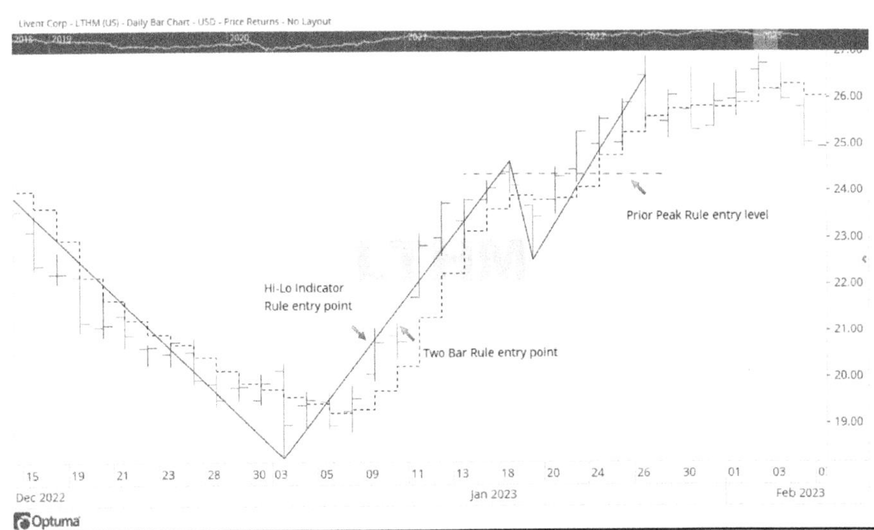

Figure 2-12

Livent (LTHM) entry points

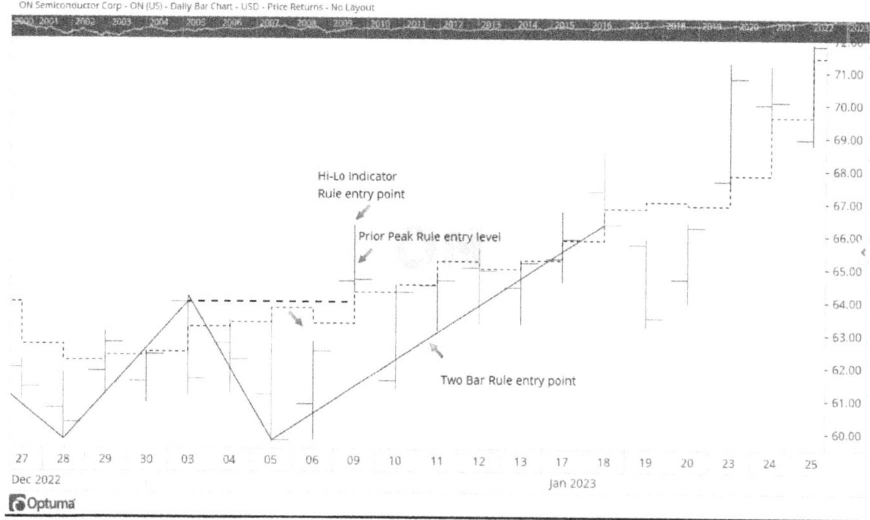

Figure 2-13

ON Semiconductor (ON) entry points

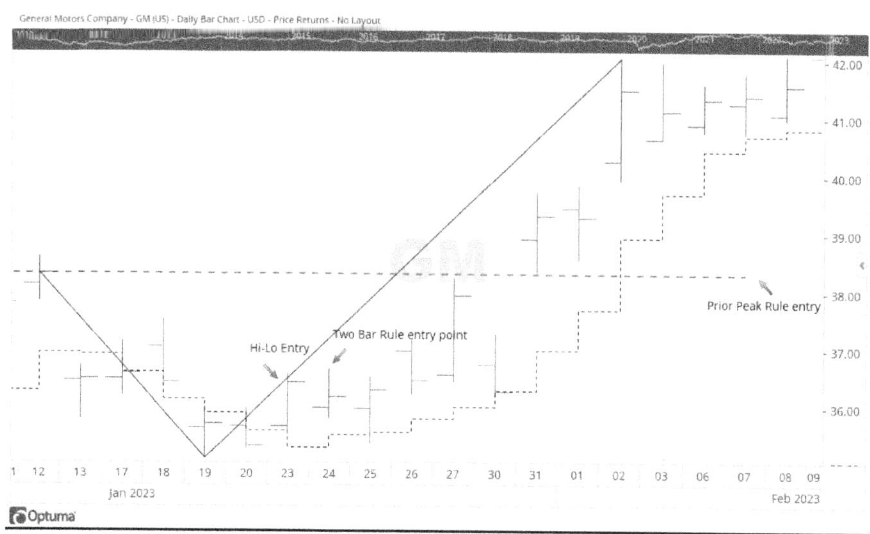

Figure 2-14

General Motors (GM) entry points

CHAPTER 3
RONDINONE'S SYMMETRICS TREND

Joe Rondinone used the course material provided by W.D. Gann to advance the concept of *Symmetrics*. Search on-line using this term and you may well stumble upon some of Rondinone's musings. Over the past several years I have read various books on unusual mathematical trading strategies. I have come across discussions of using the musical scale to define trade entry and exit points. I realize now that this notion extends back to W.D. Gann.

At the core of Symmetrics is the musical scale; in particular the major scale. A common major scale in music is the C major scale which comprises notes C, D, E, F, G, A, B. W.D. Gann focused on the C major scale because other major scales such as D major, for example, would comprise notes and sharps: D, E, F#, G, A, B, C#. The C major scale is thus the cleanest and most pure scale.

A major chord consists of the first, third, and fifth notes of a major scale. In the C major scale, the C major chord would be C, E, G. To the human ear, this chord is pleasant sounding.

Figure 3-1

Gold futures and the Symmetrics trend lines

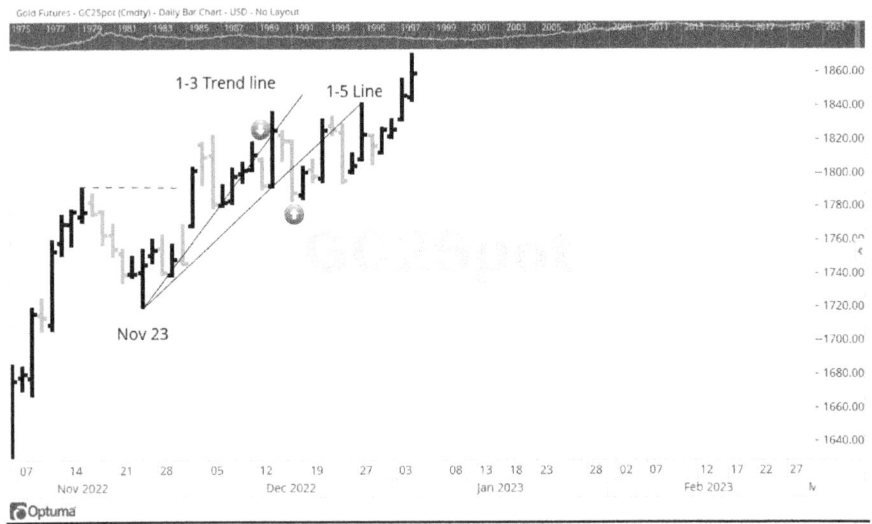

Figure 3-2

Gold futures and the Symmetrics trend lines

W.D. Gann devised a strategy of creating charts with rectangles. That is, instead of a simple vertical bar to denote price action for a time period, he widened the vertical bars slightly to make them look like rectangles. When a swing valley price point was noted on a chart, Gann numbered this price rectangle as number 1. He assigned successive integer numbers to the rectangles that followed.

He then drew a trend line connecting the lower right corner of rectangle 1 to the lower right corner of rectangle 3. This he called the *1-3 trend line*. He next drew a trend line connecting the lower right corner of rectangle 1 to the lower right corner of the rectangle for price point 5. This he called the *1-5 trend line*. When a swing peak was noted on a chart, Gann numbered that price rectangle as number 1. He assigned successive integer numbers to the rectangles that followed. He then drew a trend line connecting the upper right corner of the swing peak rectangle to the upper right corner of the rectangle for price point 3. He did likewise for price point 5.

Gann regarded these trend lines as *true trend lines* and therefore good decision-making tools. Gann advised that a violation of a 1-3 line was something to pay attention to. A violation of a 1-5 line was a more serious matter.

Figure 3-1 illustrates price action on Gold futures for the last couple months of 2022. November 3 delivered a valley swing point. From there, Gold prices started to advance. In Figure 3-1, I have instructed the Optuma software to make wider bars. The lighter shaded bars represent down days (closing price less than opening price), the darker shaded bars are up days (closing price above opening price).

From the November 3, swing point, I have drawn a 1-3 trendline and a 1-5 trendline.

A trader taking a long position because of the November 3 swing, would have applied one of Gann's rules from the previous chapter. At the far

Figure 3-3

Wheaton Precious Metals (TSX: WPM) and Symmetrics

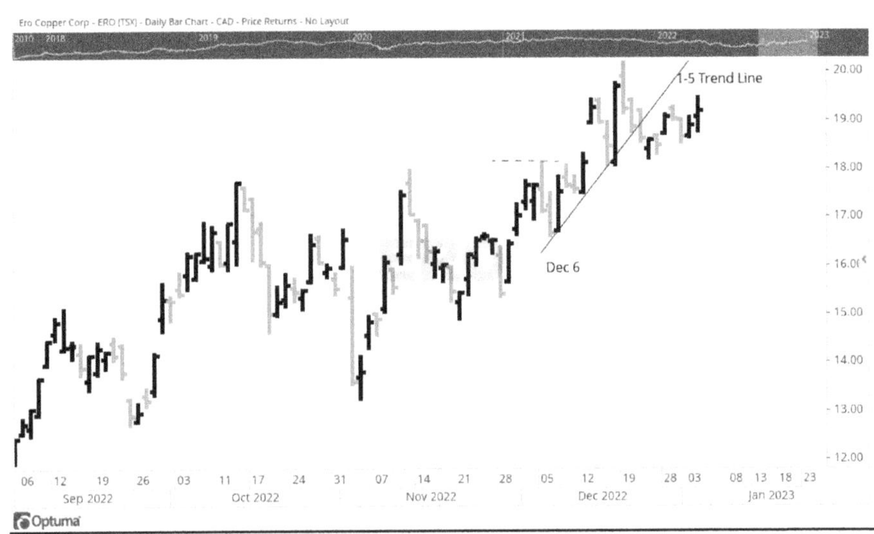

Figure 3-4

ERO Copper (TSX: ERO) and Symmetrics

left of this chart one can see a price peak point at near $1680. Following Gann's Prior Peak rule, a trader would have implemented a long trade on November 4. The next day, November 5, would have provided a total of three price bars and an opportunity to draw the 1-3 trend line connecting the lower right corners of the three price rectangles. A couple days later a 1-5 trend line could have been added. A trader, now with a long position in Gold, would be hopefully trailing the long position with a stop loss order. Moreover, he would have been alert to price bars exhibiting a closing price that violated one or both trend lines. That violation came on November 14 when Gold closed under the 1-3 trend line. The next day, November 15, Gold prices closed below the 1-5 trend line. The November 15 price bar also proved to be a peak swing point.

Continuing on with the Gold trading scenario, Figure 3-2 shows that November 23 provided another swing point for a long trade. A trader would have used one of Gann's rules from the previous chapter to define the trade entry point. Assuming the Gann Prior Peak rule was used, the long trade would have been taken as price surpassed the dashed line ($1792). Meantime, the 1-3 and 1-5 trend lines could have been drawn. On December 12, price action violated the 1-3 trend line; the trader would have exited the long position. The profitability of the trade would have been minimal. On December 15, price action violated the 1-5 trend line. A trader following this line would have closed his long position at a small profit gain.

Canadian-based Wheaton Precious Metals is a streaming company that finances start-up mining projects in return for a royalty of the metals mined. The received metals are then sold as management deems prudent. Figure 3-3 illustrates the late 2022 daily price action on the stock.

On September 1 2022, a swing valley point was formed. An over-eager trader with no set of rules to follow taking a long position would have initially realized a gain on the trade. But then at September 12, price action doubled back on itself. The trader, had be held on to his position, would have been dismayed at the false start. That same trader following Gann's Prior Peak rule, would have waited for the prior peak of August 10 to be taken out. By exercising some patience and waiting for the prior price peak to be taken out, the entire false start / doubling back scenario would have been avoided. A simple rule, courtesy of W.D. Gann, can save a lot of emotional anguish.

On September 26, another swing valley point made an appearance. A trader aiming to take a long position would have identified as a trade entry point the September 12 prior peak of $44.22. As price began to work its way higher, the trader would have been able to add a 1-5 trend line to the chart. On September 30, a long position would have been taken as price passed the prior peak at $44.22. Following the rule of watching for closing price to violate the 1-5 trend line, the long position would have been held until October 5 when a stop loss would have been triggered. The gain on the trade would have been in the range of $2. On, say, 500 shares that would have represented a decent reward for 3 days of holding the shares.

ERO Copper (TSX:ERO, NYSE:ERO) is a Canadian-based mining company that is mining a substantial Copper deposit in Brazil. As Figure 3-4 shows, a swing point appeared on December 6. A trader following the Prior Peak rule would have been eyeing $18.15 as an entry point for a long trade. December 12 would have provided the entry opportunity as well as a chance to draw a 1-5 trend line on the chart. The next day, price action gapped higher. The Symmetrics method advises to be wary when gaps start appearing on charts, for a trend change could be imminent. In this case, the gap was filled over the next couple sessions and then price pushed higher again. At some point, the trader would have exited the long position and made as much as $1.50 per share profit; not bad for a 9-day trade.

The markets today are certainly more volatile than when Joe Rondinone and W.D. Gann were trading in 1955. This explains why in these examples,

I have used the 1-5 trend line instead of the 1-3 trend line. Gann had also advised Rondinone about the 1-8 trend line. The C major scale repeats itself, each time adding an octave. C, D, E, F, G, A, B leads to C, D, E, F, G, A, B again. C, E, G, and C are points 1, 3, 5, and 8. A trader willing to endure more volatility might consider drawing a 1-8 trend line along with the 1-5 trend line. If the 1-5 trend line is violated, but only slightly, the 1-8 trend line might extend the trading horizon a few more days.

CHAPTER 4
THE TREND ACCORDING TO GARTLEY

Harold Gartley was born in New Jersey in 1899. He attended the Newark Technical School and then New York University where he received his Bachelor's Degree in Commercial Science followed by a Master's Degree in Business Administration. When Harold Gartley was 12 years old, he got a summer job on the floor of the New York Stock Exchange as an odd-lot runner. It was his job to run around on the NYSE floor looking for buyers and sellers of odd-lots of shares needed to fill orders. For example, if Gartley's employer received an order to buy 210 shares of ABC Company, his employer would easily fill the even lot 200-share part of the order. It was then young Harold's job to find a trader on the NYSE floor who wanted to sell him the 10 shares of ABC stock to complete the 210-share odd-lot order.

He was so enamored with the operation of the NYSE he went on to use his University education to carve out a successful career as a trader and financial advisor. In 1936, he created a home-study course entitled *Profits in the Stock Market*. This course material established Harold Gartley as an authority on the subject of market trends. The course material was purchased by Lambert Gann Publishing from Gartley's widow in the early 1980s and re-published in hard cover book format under the title *Profits in the Stock Market.*

The Major Trend

Gartley focused on two trends: the *major* and the *intermediate*. In his home-study course, Gartley maintained the major trend was best viewed by overlaying a price chart with a longer-term moving average such as a 200-day average. Times when price action was above the 200-day average represented a bullish major trend. Times when price action was below the 200-day average represented a bearish major trend. In his course material, he described how a bull market will commence at depressed lows and progress to a speculative climax. Panic then sets in as everyone tries to sell at once. Prices persistently decline as corporate earnings fall. Eventually, there will be a moment of capitulation as investors throw in the towel and abandon the stock market. This sets the stage for the next bull market. The difference between Gartley's era and today is the speed at which markets and individual market sectors switch from bullish to bearish and back to bullish again.

Gartley's study of market data suggested to him that from 1897 to 1932, major-trending bull markets lasted from 15 to 73 months following the completion of a major-trending bear market. As for amplitude, he observed that bull markets gained between 26% to 339%. This latter skewed figure represented the case in the roaring bull market of the 1920s. He found that 80% gains were common over the 1897-1932 period. He observed that bear markets lasted from 11 to 34 months and had an average amplitude of around 32%.

I have examined monthly chart data for the Dow Jones Average from 1942 onwards. My analysis suggests that the ups and downs of the market (bull markets and bear markets) have become more frequent over time.

I attribute this to an increasing number of market participants and an increasing number of traders using short-term quantitative algorithmic models. Ignoring a couple extreme points in the overall data set, the remainder of the data suggests bull markets since 1942 have been 15 to 42 months. As for amplitude, data suggests bull market amplitude since 1942 has been 23% to 250%. The data shows that bear markets since 1942 have lasted from 3 to 22 months with several of the data points being single digit time spans. The data shows the amplitude on half of the bear markets since 1942 to have been less than 35%.

For all the stocks, commodities, ETFs, and indices I follow, I still use Gartley's approach of a bullish trend being defined as price action being above the 200-day average. I still use his approach of a bearish trend being defined as price action being below the 200-day average. However, I have come to expect a great deal more volatility than what Gartley would have encountered in the 1930s and 1940s.

Figure 4-1 illustrates a daily chart of the Dow Jones Industrial Average from early 2020 to November 2022. The chart has been overlaid with the 200-day moving average.

The Dow Jones Average broke beneath its 200-day average in late February 2020. This was mere days after it became apparent that a nasty virus was poised to cause global health issues. Fear of COVID-19 bearing down on North America brought a swift end to a 13-month bull market. The Dow Jones Average broke beneath the 200-day average and the trend shifted to bearish.

As governments around the globe started to pile stimulus money into the financial system, the market responded favorably. In early July 2020, the Dow Jones climbed above the 200-day moving average; a bullish major trend was now in place. On October 30, 2020, the Dow Jones tested the 200-day average, but did not penetrate beneath it. This was further confirmation of the voracity of the bullish trend.

Figure 4-1

Dow Jones Industrial Average with 200-day average

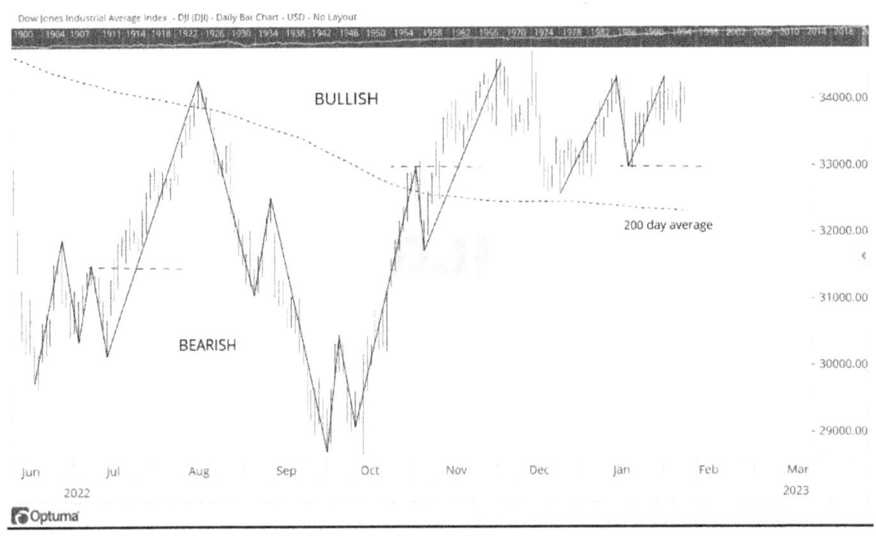

Figure 4-2

Dow Jones Industrial Average with Gann swings and Gartley major

In mid-January 2022, the Dow Jones decisively broke beneath its 200-day average. The trend had now changed from bullish to bearish. The global geopolitical playing field was about to experience a serious tilt. Russian troops were massing on the eastern border of Ukraine. The financial market was nervous. The Dow Jones staged a rally attempt to get back above the 200-day average in early February, but the rally could not sustain itself. By late February 2022, the Dow Jones had fallen 2000 points as Russian troops began their full-scale invasion. Then came confirmation from the Federal Reserve that interest rates would definitely be rising and that liquidity available in the financial system would be reduced. March and April 2022 saw two attempts at a rally, but each attempt failed to stay above the 200-day average. August and late October 2022 each saw an attempt at a trend-changing rally. Neither attempt was able to hold above the 200-day average. Finally in early November, the Dow Jones managed to climb above its 200-day average and stayed there. The market players had convinced themselves that the Federal Reserve would soon tire of raising its key lending rate. At this time of writing in early 2023, the hold on the 200-day average is by 1300 points. A few days of triple digit declines and the 200-day average could come under assault.

To add a nuance to this trend discussion, Figure 4-2 illustrates the W.D. Gann Prior Peak rule overlaid on a chart showing Gartley's 200-day average major trend.

The Gann Prior Peak method shows that a buy signal materialized in July 2022 (dashed line on the chart). This buy signal that emerged was despite the fact that the major trend according to Gartley was bearish. When buying signals emerge within a bearish major trend, a trader should remain cognizant of the bearish reality. In fact, as Figure 4-2 shows, the Dow Jones Average hit the 200-day average in August and promptly turned lower. At the right side of the chart, the Dow Jones major trend was bullish. However, price action was struggling to surpass the prior peak made in January 2023. On any buy signal materializing, a trader would have to remain cognizant that a move beneath the dashed line at the 33,000 level

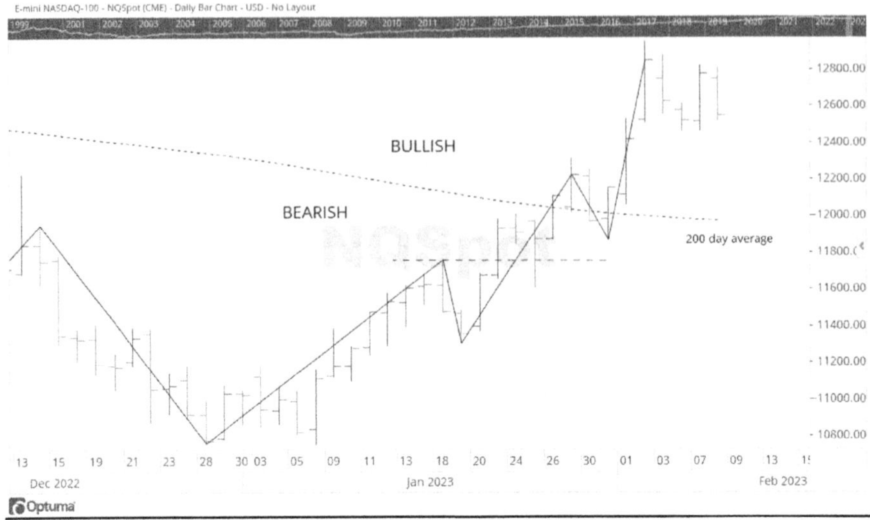

Figure 4-3

E-mini Nasdaq Average with Gann swings and Gartley major trend

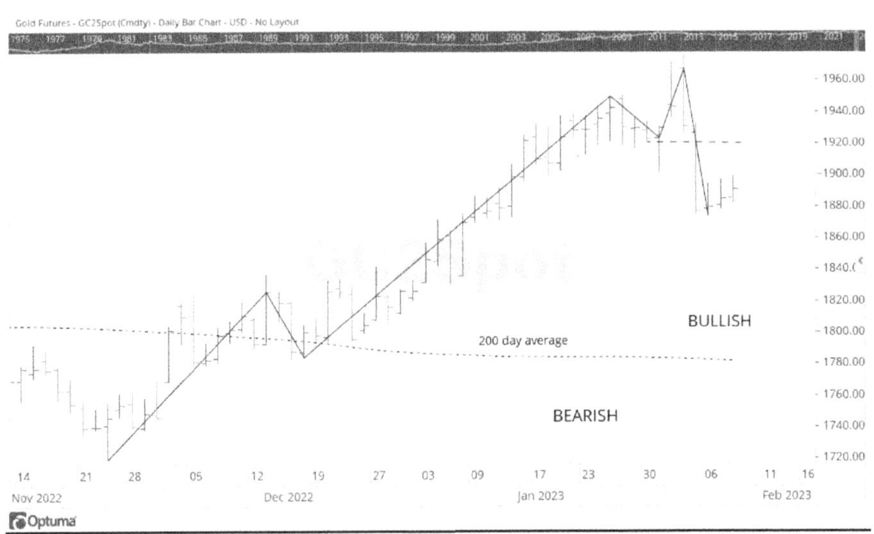

Figure 4-4

Gold futures (front month) with Gann swings and Gartley major trend

would trigger a sell signal, even though the major trend is bullish.

As another example, Figure 4-3 illustrates the E-mini Nasdaq Index with the W.D. Gann Prior Peak rule overlaid along with the Gartley 200-day average major trend. At this time of writing, a breach of the 200-day moving average will turn the major trend negative and at the same time threaten the prior swing low made on January 31, 2023. A move lower by only 300 points would bring this scenario into focus.

Figure 4-4 illustrates daily price action on front-month Gold futures. At this time of writing, price has just broken beneath a prior swing point after again failing to get above the $2000 level. This is the third time since 2011 that Gold prices have failed to surpass the $2000 per ounce level. However, at this time of writing the major bullish trend is still intact. Only a move below $1780 would shift the major trend to bearish. Is this just a pause before a renewed attempt to surpass $2000? A move above the prior swing peak at $1975 will answer this question in the affirmative.

Figure 4-5 illustrates price action on an ETF that owns a secured physical inventory of Platinum metal. The ETF is managed by a manager called GraniteShares. In late January 2023, price of this ETF fell beneath a prior swing point at the $10 level. Price action as of this time of writing is hovering precariously just above entering bearish territory. Platinum is more than just jewelry. Each year over half of the Platinum mined is used in the making of pollution-abating catalytic converters for cars, trucks and buses.

Intermediate Trend

In the early 1900s, Charles Dow (after whom the Dow Jones Average is partly named) observed that within a bull market or a bear market, there will be times when prices move counter to the bull or bear trend. These movements comprised of see-saw price action are what Gartley termed *intermediate trends*. Gartley suggested that after an intermediate movement

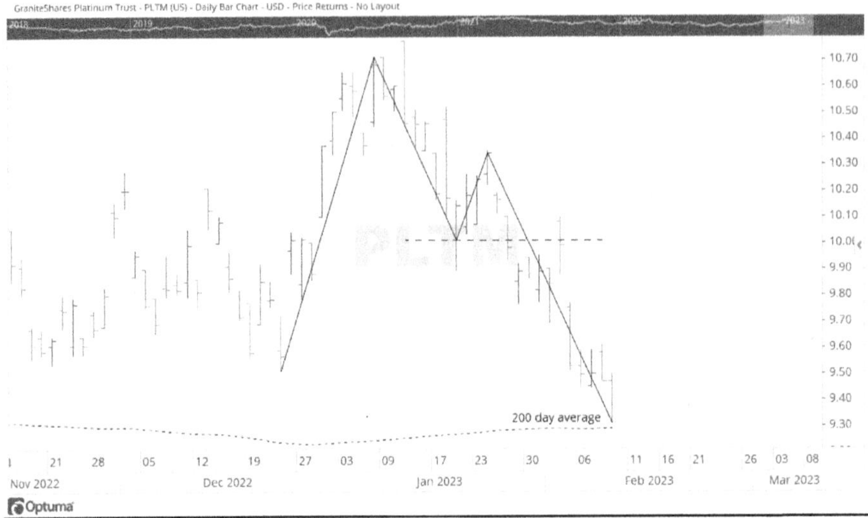

Figure 4-5

Platinum ETF with Gann swings and Gartley major trend

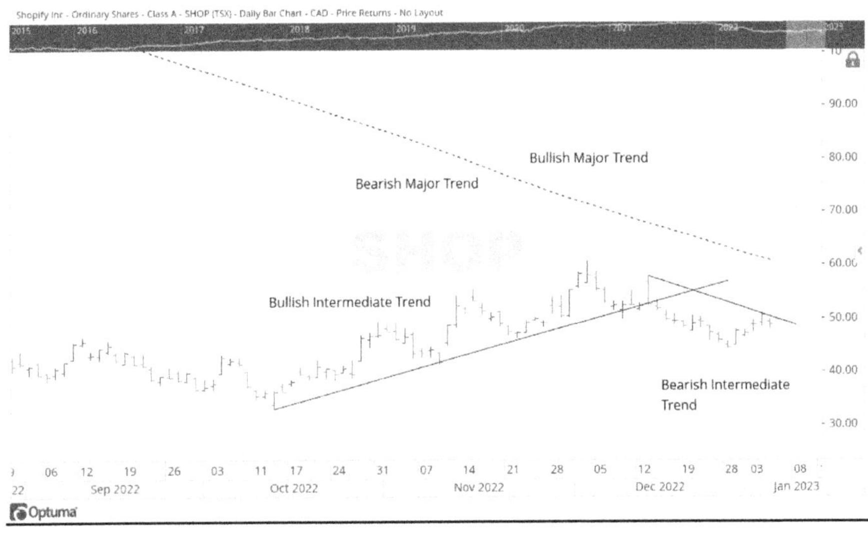

Figure 4-6

Shopify (TSX: SHOP) with Gartley trends

in one direction, it is common to observe a corrective movement of 33-66% in the opposite direction, thus creating the see-saw pattern on the price chart.

I have come to conclude that what Gartley was alluding to with his 33-66% observation is Fibonacci retracements. These retracements are based on the Fibonacci sequence. The Fibonacci sequence of numbers starts with 0, 1 and another 1. The sequence then continues such that the next term of the sequence is the sum total of the two preceding terms. This is a *recursive* sequence. The first fourteen Fibonacci sequence numbers are as follows: 1, 1, 2, 3, 5, 8, 13, 21, 34, 55, 89, 144, 233, and 377.

The values that comprise the Fibonacci sequence were in use as early as 200 B.C. by Indian poet Acharya Pingala who was studying syllabic patterns in Sanskrit poetry. Circa 1200 A.D., Italian mathematician Leonardo Bonacci (a.k.a. Fibonacci) popularized the recursive sequence using a story of a pair of rabbits generating offspring.

In addition to the recursive pattern, if one takes a number from the Fibonacci sequence and divides the number by the prior number in the sequence, the result will be close to the number 1.618. This value is what ancient Greek artists and philosophers regarded as the *Golden Mean*. Mathematicians often assign the 1.618 value the Greek letter *phi*. The inverse of the square root of phi equates to 0.786. The inverse of the square root of phi to the power 2, equates to 0.618. The inverse of the square root of phi to the power 3, equates to 0.486. The inverse of the square root of phi to the power 4, equates to 0.382. The inverse of the square root of phi to the power 6, equates to 0.236. The values 0.786, 0.618, 0.486, 0.382, and 0.236 expressed as percentages are 78.6%, 61.8%, 48.6%, 38.2%, and 23.6%. In a chart see-saw pattern, it is common to see price advance and then retreat by these percentage values.

Gartley referred to the see-saw patterns on a price chart as *cycles*. He concluded that each cycle will have two components: a component that

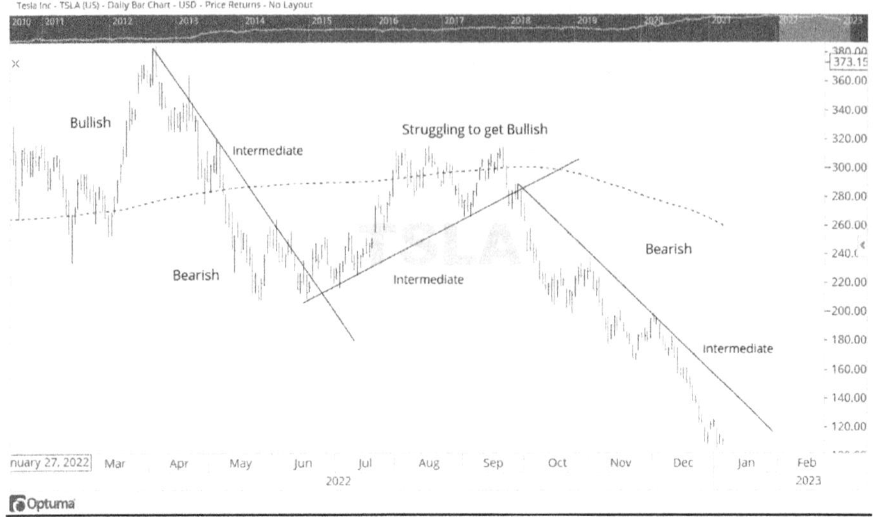

Figure 4-7

Tesla (TSLA) with Gartley trends

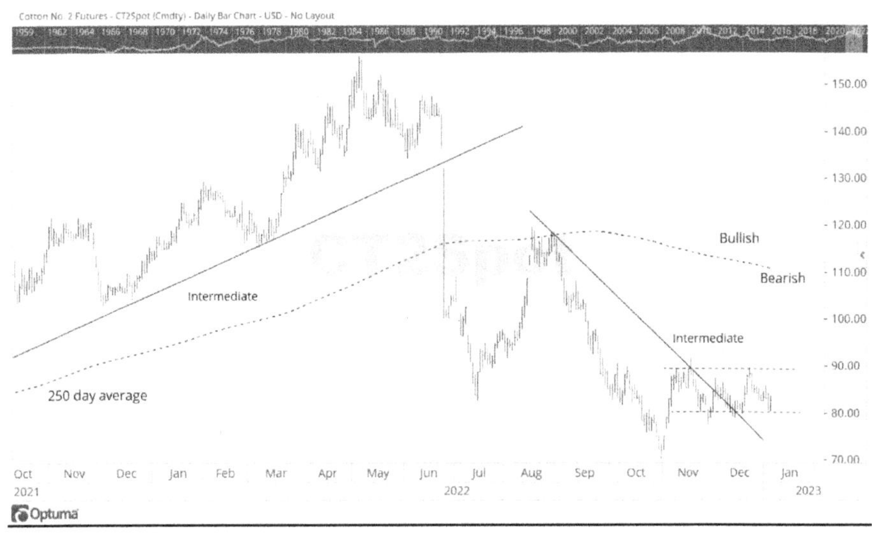

Figure 4-8

Cotton futures with Gartley trends

moves in the same direction as the prevailing major trend and a corrective component that moves counter to the direction of the major trend. Gartley said that an intermediate bullish trend comprises cycles that go from a price low to a subsequent price low. An intermediate bearish trend comprises cycles that go from a price high to a subsequent price high.

Gartley then advised to draw a line that roughly connects the sequential low points in a rising price scenario. He advised drawing a line that roughly connects the sequential high points in a rising price scenario. The resulting lines he called the *intermediate trend lines.*

To illustrate, consider the chart in Figure 4-6 of e-Commerce platform provider Shopify (TSX:SHOP). The dashed line on the chart is the 200-day average. Price action is below this long term average, hence the major trend on Shopify is bearish. Starting at a swing point in mid-October 2022, price action on Shopify started to move higher. The line from October into December connecting the series of higher lows is the intermediate trend line. Gartley would have described Shopify in late 2022 as being in a bearish major trend, but having a bullish intermediate trend. In late December, price action violated the previous low within the intermediate trend. This caused the intermediate trend to become bearish. In early January 2023, Gartley would have described Shopify as being in a bearish major trend, with a bearish intermediate trend.

The Gann Prior Peak method could also be applied to the intermediate trend line technique. Without actually adding the various swing lines to the SHOP chart in Figure 4-6, one can see that the Prior Peak approach would have yielded a series of very small trade gains within the bullish intermediate trend. Why small gains? The answer is because the stock was mired in a bearish major trend. Bearish major trends do not usually offer up copious trading rewards for the trader seeking to take long positions.

Figure 4-7 illustrates the price action of electric vehicle maker, Tesla. For traders seeking a volatile stock, TSLA will certainly deliver. In March

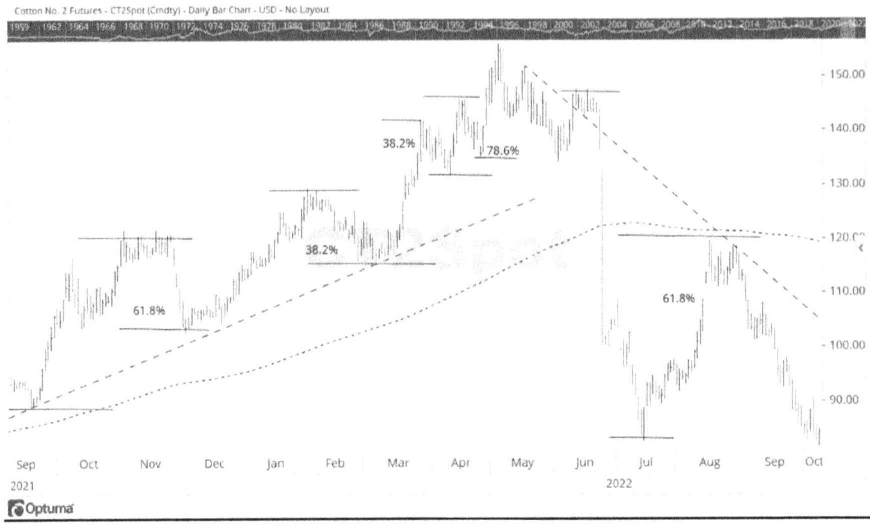

Figure 4-9

Cotton futures with Fibonacci

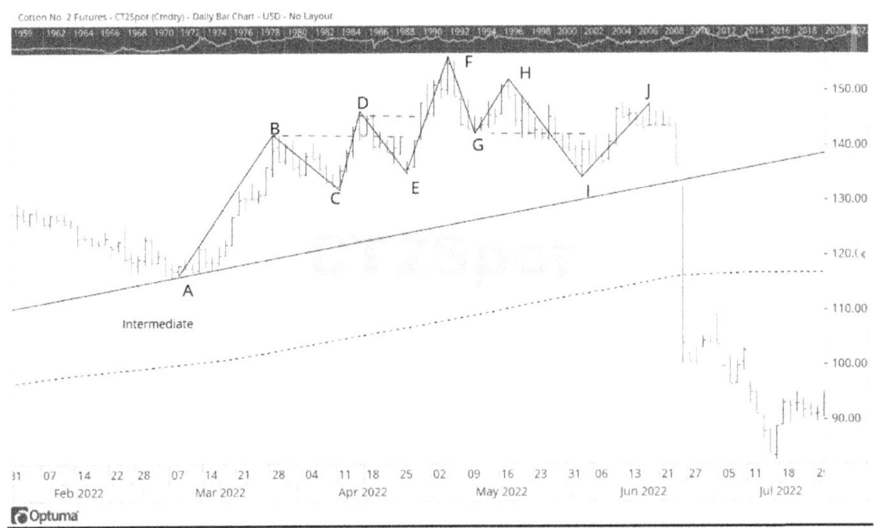

Figure 4-10

Cotton futures with Fibonacci, Gartley, and Gann

2022, price action tested the 200-day average and decided to hold above it (aside from a couple minor excursions beneath). The major trend in March 2022 was bullish. After reaching the $380 level in early April, the share price could push no higher. The intermediate trend turned bearish within the bullish trend. In May, price action violated the long term average. The intermediate trend was still bearish, but now within the context of a bearish major trend.

The intermediate trend, denoted by a series of lower tops remained in force until June when the lower top pattern came under duress. In July, the intermediate trend turned bullish within the overall bearish major trend. The bullish intermediate trend, denoted by a series of higher lows, remained intact until October when the pattern was violated. Between August and October, on three occasions, price tried to get above the long term average and into bullish major territory. Each time, the effort was unsuccessful. This was not an encouraging sign.

As of the first couple days of January 2023, the bearish intermediate pattern of lower tops was still intact. The bearish major trend was still intact. But then an unusual turn of events materialized. Just as speculation was building that Tesla was severely overpriced, on January 6, 2023, share price recorded a Fibonacci 78.6% retracement of the move from the March 2020 lows to the March 2022 highs. At this time of writing, Tesla shares have rallied a Fibonacci 48.6% retracement of the decline from March 2022 through January 2023.

As an example of how the Gartley method can be used with commodity futures, consider the Cotton futures charts in Figures 4-9 through 4-11. In late 2021, the price of cotton was rising. Price was above its 200-day average in bullish territory. The intermediate trend was bullish as well; a line could be drawn joining a series of rising lows. In May 2022, cotton prices suddenly slumped as demand for cotton fabrics fell in response to supply chain dislocations. At least, this was the story that circulated amongst commodity analysts. What this story failed to consider was

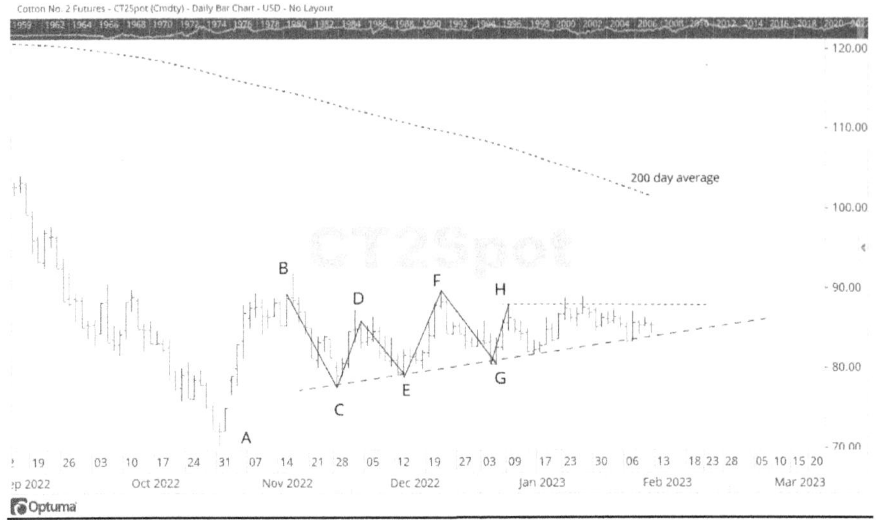

Figure 4-11

Cotton futures with Gartley, Gann, and Fibonacci

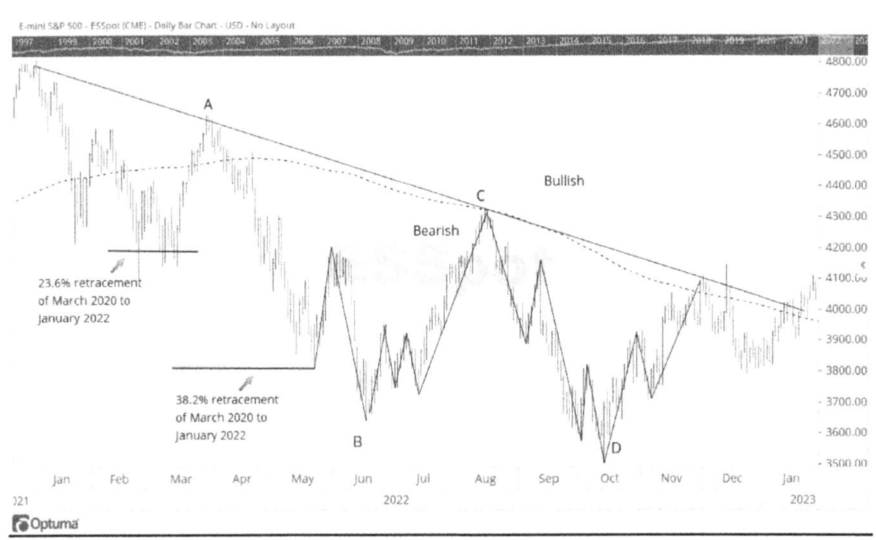

Figure 4-12

E-mini S&P 500 with Gann swings, Gartley trends, and Fibonacci

the Fibonacci element. Between February 2011 and February 2016, the price of cotton declined. The price gain from the February 2016 low to the May 2022 peak was a Fibonacci 61.8% retracement of the 2011 to 2016 decline. Price topping out at this level was not a guarantee, but it should not have come as a shock to traders either. Unfortunately, it seems that few were applying Fibonacci mathematics to the cotton market.

So swift was the drop from the $1.55 per pound price peak that within two trading sessions, cotton had fallen into a bearish major trend. In August, cotton prices tried to claw their way back above the long-term moving average. But it was not to be. Price tested the average but could not muster the strength to get above it. The bearish major trend remained intact and a bearish intermediate trend took form. In early February 2023, the US cotton crop in Texas was suffering from drought. Demand for cotton fabrics was down. Meanwhile, other growing areas around the globe were poised to harvest decent crops. Cotton futures prices were unsure of which way to move and lapsed into a sideways pattern on the price chart shown in Figure 4-11.

The moves within the see-saw bullish intermediate trend of cotton futures from September 2021 through to the May 2022 top provide an opportunity to examine the magnitude of the see-saw moves in the context of Fibonacci retracement percentages. As Figure 4.9 illustrates, the various advances and retreats were in accordance with Fibonacci mathematics. Even the steep drop and counter-trend rally in June-August 2022 followed Fibonacci mathematics.

The moves within the see-saw bullish intermediate trend of cotton futures from September 2021 through to the May 2022 top provide an opportunity to examine the magnitude of the see-saw moves in the context of Fibonacci retracement percentages. As Figure 4.9 illustrates, the various advances and retreats were in accordance with Fibonacci mathematics. Even the steep drop and counter-trend rally in June-August 2022 followed Fibonacci mathematics.

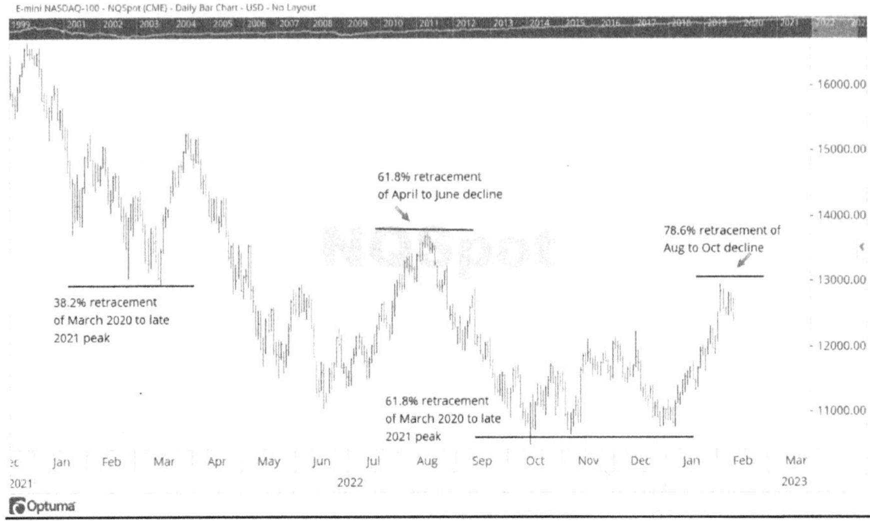

Figure 4-13

E-mini Nasdaq with Gann swings, Gartley trends, and Fibonacci

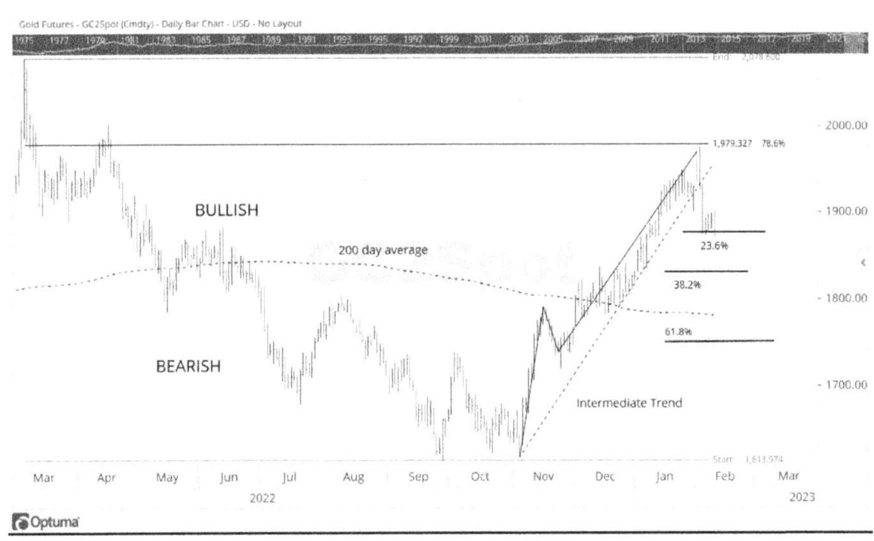

Figure 4-14

Gold futures with Gann swings, Gartley trends, and Fibonacci

The cotton market generally moved in a sideways pattern from November 2022 through early 2023. An application of a Gartley intermediate trend line, Gann Prior Peak methodology, and Fibonacci mathematics reveals more than just a sideways pattern as Figure 4-11 shows.

The move from B to C is 61.8% of A-B. The move from C to D is 61.8% of B-C. The move from D to E is 78.6% of C-D. The move E-F is 100% of B-C. The E-F move is also very nearly a 1.486 extension of D-E. The move F-G is 78.6% of E-F. The move G-H is 78.6% of F-G. An alert trader watching price move from E to F could have taken a long position in cotton futures as price surpassed the swing peak at D. At this time of writing, price will have to surpass 88 cents (point H) to trigger a buy signal.

Let's now consider some further examples that incorporate Fibonacci mathematics:

Figure 4-12 illustrates daily price action on the E-mini S&P 500 Index. The quantity C-D is a Fibonacci 78.6% fraction of the quantity A-B. By late February 2022, the S&P had retraced a Fibonacci 23.6% of the overall move from the March 2020 lows to the January 2022 peak. By May 2022, the S&P had retraced a Fibonacci 38.2% of the overall move from the March 2020 low to the January 2022 peak. The move from B to C was a 61.8% retracement of the A-B; not quite enough to surpass the 200-day average and turn the major trend positive.

Figure 4-13 illustrates daily price action on the E-mini Nasdaq Index. After recording a significant high in late 2021, the Nasdaq declined. The support that appeared to be forming in February-March 2022 was at a 38.2% Fibonacci retracement of the overall move from the March 2020 low to the late 2021 peak. The ensuing counter-trend rally turned out to be a 61.8% retracement of the January to March decline. The failure of the rally to press beyond 61.8% then resulted in a drawdown into the June 2022 timeframe. A counter-trend rally that then lasted into the

August timeframe was a 61.8% retracement of the April through June decline. The failure of the rally to press beyond 61.8% then resulted in a drawdown into the October 2022 timeframe.

The lows made in the October through December 2022 timeframe are very likely a solid support level given that this level is a Fibonacci 61.8% retracement of the overall move from the March 2020 low to the late 2021 peak. A full Fibonacci 78.6% retracement would take the Nasdaq to the 8700 level.

At the right side of the chart, price action on the Nasdaq is struggling to move higher, having made a Fibonacci 78.6% retracement of the August through October 2022 decline.

As another example, consider Gold futures. Figure 4-14 illustrates Gold futures prices from March 2022 through February 2023.

In March 2022, Gold price tried to surpass and stay above the $2000 per ounce level. The valiant effort failed and Gold prices began backsliding. In May 2022, price fell beneath the 200-day average, shifting the major trend to bearish. Numerous efforts to get back above the 200-day average all failed and by October 2022 Gold price was at the $1600 per ounce level. Gold then did an abrupt turn and came back into fashion as a hedge against global uncertainty. This about-turn was not a random, chance event. It came at a Fibonacci 48.6% retracement of the move from the 2018 significant lows (around $1200 per ounce) and the March 2022 highs at just over $2000 per ounce.

In early February 2023, Gold hit another turning point at just under $2000 per ounce. This was a Fibonacci 78.6% retracement of the move from March 2022 through the October-November lows. Along the way to making this high, Gold price adhered to a Gartley intermediate trend line. In late December 2022, the intermediate and major trends were both bullish. By late January 2023, Gold price had retraced 23.6% of the move from the October-November lows. The intermediate trend line had been broken. A 61.8% retracement would take Gold price to beneath $1800 per ounce and into bearish major trend territory.

Next, consider the price action of the 10-Year Treasury Notes as illustrated in Figure 4-15. From March 2022 through January 2023 the 10-Year Notes exhibited a bearish major trend and a bearish intermediate trend. The price move above the intermediate trend line in early 2023 quickly came under threat and receded back beneath the intermediate trend line. Two attempts to surpass the 200-day average were also both unsuccessful.

Figure 4-15 has been labeled with points A, B, C, D, and E. The move from B to C was a Fibonacci 48.6% retracement of the move from A to B. The move from C to D was a 48.6% retracement of the move from B to C. Point D aligns to the 23.6% retracement of the A to B move. At this time of writing, price action has retraced 78.6% of the D to E move.

It is further interesting to note that point E surpassed the prior swing point at C. A trader strictly following the Gann Prior Peak rule would have experienced prices rolling over to create a losing trade. A more prudent approach would have been one of waiting to see if price could surpass the 200-day average. While it is easy to comment on this in hindsight, this 10-Year Treasury example underscores the risk element in trading.

I will conclude the discussion of Gartley's work with one final observation. Gartley suggested that a 28-day moving average be applied to charts. He offered little in the way of explanation of why he chose the number 28. Figure 4-16 illustrates price action on the E-mini S&P 500. In January 2023, as price moved above the 200-day average, the intermediate trend (dashed descending line) also changed to bullish. Figure 4-16 has been fitted with a 28-day average. I can see no immediate benefit from this average. I have decided that his major and intermediate trends are sufficient for my trading. I do not use the 28-day average.

Figure 4-15

10-Year Treasury Notes with Gann swings, Gartley trends, and Fibonacci

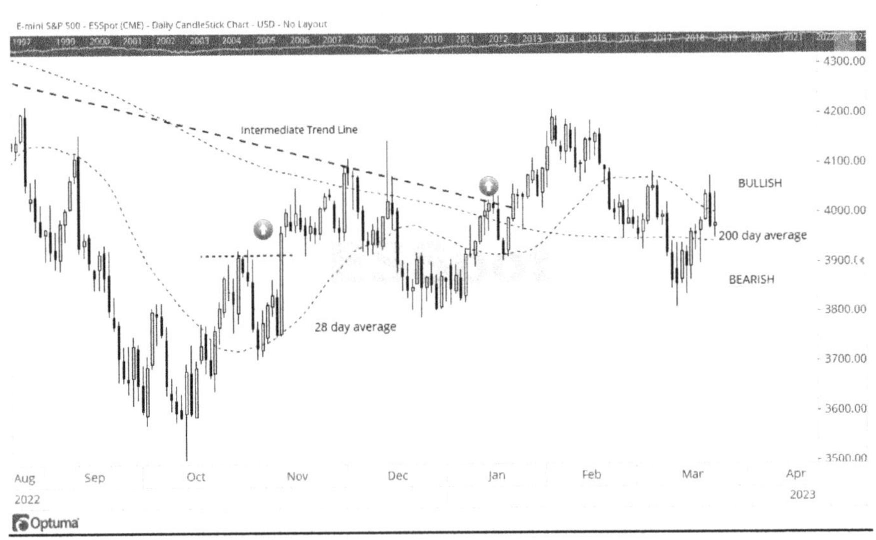

Figure 4-16

E-mini S&P 500 with Gann swings and Gartley trends

To Sum Up

The major trend of a stock, commodity, or index is defined by the price relative to a long term average, such as the 200-day average. When prices are trading above the long term average, the major trend is bullish. When prices are trading below the long term average, the major trend is bearish.

Major trends are comprised of both bullish and bearish intermediate trends. Price action of an intermediate trend will move in cycles. Each cycle will comprise a component where price travels in the direction of the major trend, and a corrective component where price travels counter to the major trend direction. Positive intermediate trends will display a series of higher price lows. Bearish intermediate trends will display a series of lower price highs. The intermediate trend will resemble a see-saw pattern. The advance and decline legs of the see-saw will almost always conform to Fibonacci retracement values.

When Gartley's trend work is used in conjunction with Gann's swing peaks and valleys methodology, the result is a powerful strategy for traders to embrace.

Throughout this chapter, the use of moving averages has been highlighted. A deeper examination of moving averages is now required. Can they be used to help a trader decide when to buy and when to sell? The next Chapter reveals more.

Addendum

Just as this book was to go to press, a banking crisis suddenly materialized. Several regional banks in the USA were taken over by regulators. At the same time, in Switzerland, Credit Suisse was given a bail out package and merged with Union Bank of Switzerland. Figures 4-17 through 4-19 illustrate the effects of this crisis on the E-mini Nasdaq, the E-mini S&P 500, and Gold futures.

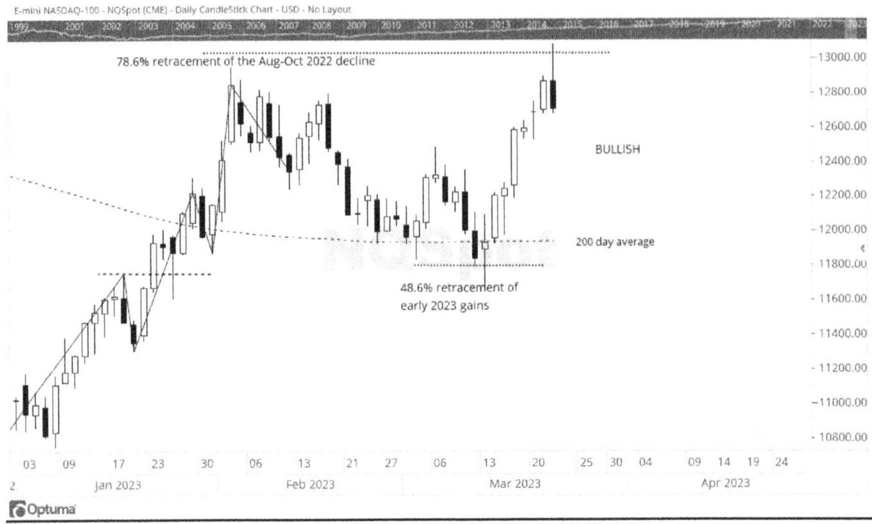

Figure 4-17

E-mini Nasdaq, Gartley, and Fibonacci

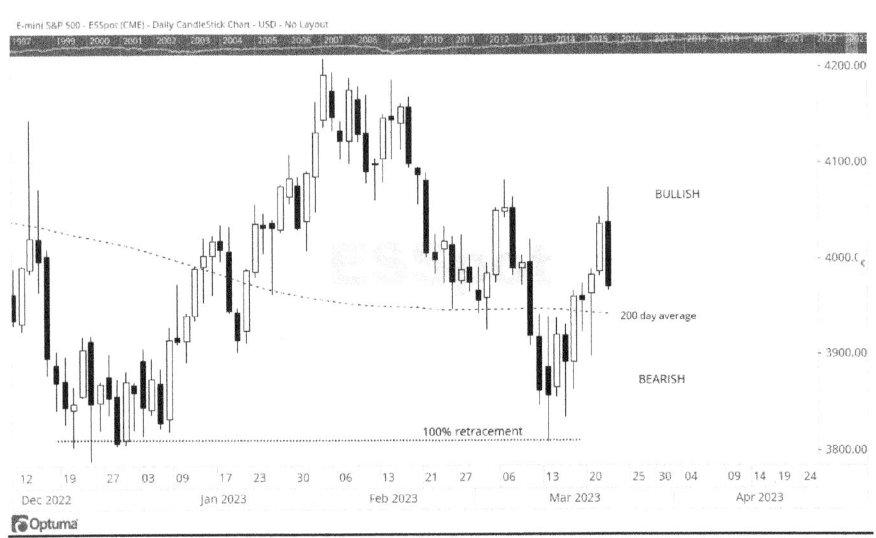

Figure 4-18

E-mini S&P 500, Gartley, and Fibonacci

The E-mini Nasdaq retraced only 48.6% of its 2023 gains and only briefly penetrated the 200-day average.

The E-mini S&P 500 retraced 100% of gains of 2023, falling beneath the 200-day average. News of depositor guarantees brought relief to the market and a move back above the 200-day average.

By late February, Gold had retraced 48.6% of its November 2022 to January 2023 gains. Gold appeared as though it was headed for a violation of its 200-day average. News of the bank failures halted the downward momentum. Gold powered higher to record a 78.6% retracement of its march through October 2022 decline.

Figure 4-19

Gold futures, Gartley, and Fibonacci

CHAPTER 5

THE MATHEMATICS OF AVERAGES

An Average – What is it?

The sequential price bars that make up a stock, commodity, or index chart can be thought of as creating a *signal*. The simple definition of a signal is: *something that conveys notice or warning*. If sequential price bars exhibit higher prices, the notice that is being conveyed is that there are more buyers than sellers. Market participants are seeking to accumulate the stock, commodity, or index in question. If sequential price bars exhibit lower prices, the notice that is being conveyed is that there are more sellers than buyers. Market participants are seeking to accumulate the stock, commodity, or index in question.

In order to properly interpret the signal, price action has to be judged relative to a number or to a statistic. This leads to the field of signal processing. Taking a descriptor from the field of signal processing, an average is a *low-pass filter*. That is, an average is an easy way; a low-pass way, of dividing a stream of numbers (a signal) into smaller or larger categories; or perhaps good and bad categories. There are many mathematical ways of creating the low-pass filter.

Static Average

An average is the sum total of a group of n numbers divided by n. Within a price bar or candlestick, an average could be as simple as the sum total of a candlestick's high and low prices (n=2) divided by 2. An average could be the sum total of a bar's high, low, and close (n=3) divided by 3. An average could be extended to be the sum total of the values of a series of n price bars divided by n. This is a *static average*, at one moment in time. But the financial markets are not a static mechanism.

Simple Moving Average

The financial markets are a dynamic signal generating system. Every trading session will add another price bar or candlestick to a daily chart. Every five trading sessions will create enough data to add another bar or candlestick to a weekly chart. Every hour will add another bar or candlestick to an hourly chart.

To keep pace with the dynamism of the markets, an alternative to static averages must be used.

Suppose one calculated a static average for a series of n price bars. Once the next data bar ($n+1$) in succession becomes available, the very first price bar in the series could be ignored. The sum total of a desired number of n bars or candlesticks would be added and divided by n. This constantly changing average calculation is called a simple moving average. All price bars or candlesticks are deemed to be of equal importance in the calculation of sum total divided by n. There are several ways of calculating the value of each individual price bar or candlestick. The value could be (high + low)/2; the value could be (high + low + close)/3; the value could be (open + high + low +close)/4; or the value could be a unique construct like the Heiken-Ashi.

Consider the chart in Figure 5-1 which illustrates price performance of the US Dollar Index from mid-2021 through November 2022. The chart has been fitted with a 200-day moving average. The prevailing major trend on the US Dollar Index is bullish and has been so since June 11, 2021 when the daily candlestick bar exhibited a (high + low + close)/3 value that was above the 200-day moving average value on that date. In keeping with the low-pass filter analogy described at the start of this chapter, the price candlesticks prior to June 11, 2021 were categorized as bearish. The candlesticks after June 11, 2021 are categorized as bullish.

The intermediate trend is shown as two solid line segments on Figure 5-1. Recall that according to Harold Gartley, the intermediate trend in a rising market is characterized by a series of cycles, each with a higher low. The lows can be joined by a line or lines. A closer examination of the rising bottoms in Figure 5-1 shows that the first cycle of the intermediate trend ran from June to February 2022. The next cycle ran from February 2022 to November 2022. Price beyond November 2022 failed to generate a higher low. This signaled a shift to a bearish intermediate trend on November 3, 2022. This bearish trend unfolded within the confines of a bullish major trend until December 2022 when price crossed under the 200-day moving average. The US Dollar was then in a bearish intermediate trend within a bearish major trend.

As Figure 5-2 shows, the bearish intermediate trend held until February 2023. An effort to potentially move through the 200-day average failed in March 2023 and the bearish intermediate trend again came into focus.

What is n ?

There is no hard and fast rule for what *n* could or should be in moving average calculations. The investment industry has adopted the values of

Figure 5-1

US Dollar Index daily candlestick chart

Figure 5-2

US Dollar Index daily candlestick chart with 28-day average

18-days, 50-days and 200-days as being the generally accepted n values for calculating averages. Many software programs will come with these being the default values. While I make full use of the 200-day average for discerning the major trend, I do not necessarily follow the 18-day or 50-day default values. I have a fascination with recursive sequence numbers. If I am going to use an n value other than the software program default values, I will use a *Fibonacci number* or a *Lucas number*.

The Fibonacci sequence is not the only recursive mathematical sequence that has been popularized. In the late 1880s, French mathematician Eduard Lucas created a recursive sequence (a given term is the sum of the two prior terms) that has come to be called the *Lucas sequence*: 2, 1, 3, 4, 7, 11, 18, 29, 47, 76, 123, 199, 322, 521, 843…and so on. Compare this sequence to the Fibonacci sequence: 1, 1, 2, 3, 5, 8, 13, 21, 34, 55, 89, 144, 233, 377, and so on.

When configuring charts in a software platform with averages, traders and investors may wish to consider deviating from standard default settings and using Fibonacci or Lucas numbers.

The Exponential Moving Average

The simple moving average gives equal consideration to all of the n price bars or candlesticks. If the price bars or candlesticks exhibit volatility across time, the question becomes, should each of the price bar data points be treated equally when it comes to calculating a moving average? What would happen if more weighting (more emphasis) was placed on more recent data points? This is the concept of an *Exponential Moving Average (EMA)*.

The *EMA* formula is:

$$EMA\,(n) = [(\text{Day } n \text{ data point} - \text{Day } n\text{-}1 \text{ EMA}) \times \text{"multiplier"}] +$$
$$(\text{Day } n\text{-}1 \text{ EMA})$$

The "multiplier" term in the formula is calculated as $2/(n+1)$;

Figure 5-3

US Dollar Index with simple and exponential averages

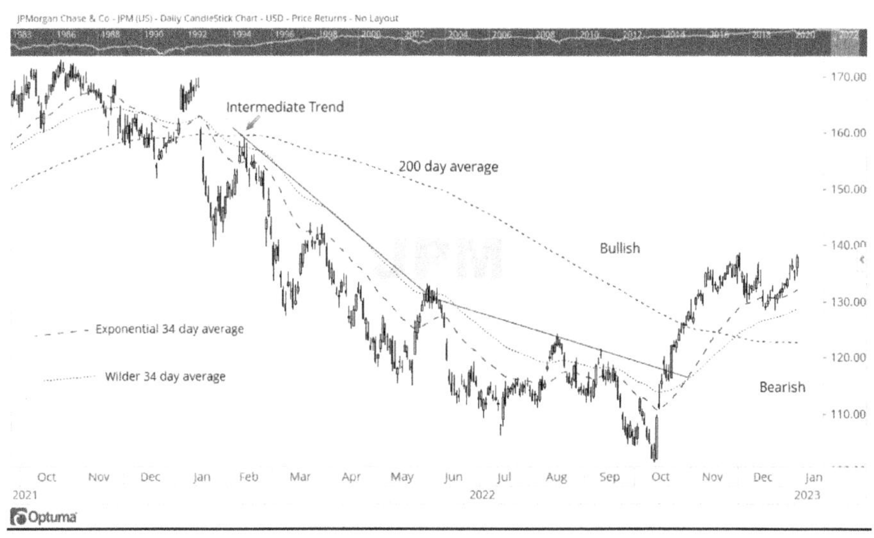

Figure 5-4

J.P. Morgan (JPM) daily chart with Exponential and Wilder

where *n* is the number of days desired in the
Exponential Moving Average.

Suppose one was interested in a 28-day *EMA*. Taking *n* to be 28, the multiplier is 2/(28 + 1) = 0.0690. Because one does not yet know the Day *n-1 EMA*, the formula demands that one start by making it equal to the 28-day simple moving average.

Figure 5-3 illustrates a 28-period (n=28) simple moving average (dotted line), and a 28-period exponential moving average (dashed line) applied to a daily chart of the US Dollar Index. The two averages provide a similar early warning of an intermediate trend change.

Wilder Moving Average

In the early 1980s, trader J. Welles Wilder created a series of technical chart indicators. One of them was his version of a moving average which he called the *Wilder Moving Average*. His approach was the same as that for the Exponential Moving Average, except Wilder used a multiplier of 1/*n* instead of the EMA multiplier of 2/(*n*+1).

The daily chart of J.P. Morgan (NYSE:JPM) in Figure 5-4 has been overlaid with a 34-period exponential moving average and a 34-period Wilder moving average. The two averages are very close to one another; the difference being the calculation of the multiplier value.

The 1980s decade was a fertile time in the application of mathematics to stock market and commodity futures trading thanks to the introduction of simple desktop computers. During my days in engineering school in the early 1980s, we were introduced to a machine called the Commodore 64 with its 5-inch floppy disc. We were also taught computer languages like Fortran and Cobol that could perform mathematical operations on arrays of data. J. Welles Wilder was an active stock trader. He was also an engineer in the aerospace industry and was well versed in the use of

Figure 5-5

J.P. Morgan (JPM) with weighted and exponential averages

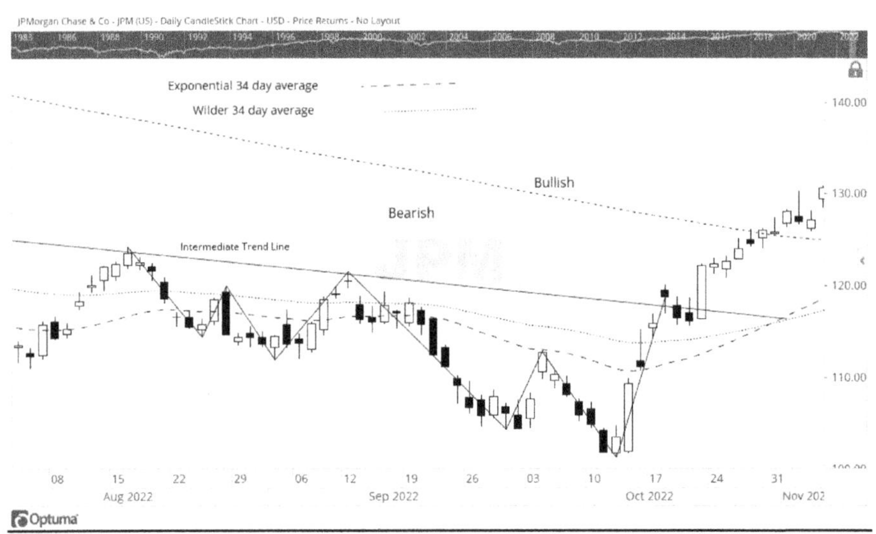

Figure 5-6

J.P. Morgan (JPM) with averages and swings

computers and programming languages. The rudimentary computers and programming languages of the day allowed him to efficiently test and develop indicators such as the Wilder moving average.

However, as the coming chapters will indicate, just because a trader developed a new chart indicator did not mean the indicator worked well under all market price movements.

The Weighted Moving Average

Another way of calculating an average while placing emphasis on the more recent data points is to compute a *Weighted Moving Average (WMA)*.

The period selected for the moving average is assigned weightings (factors).

For example, if a 34-day weighted moving average is required, the data point on day 34 is assigned a factor of 34, the data point on day 33 is assigned a factor of 33, the data point on day 32 is assigned a factor of 32 and so on with the data point on day 1 being assigned a factor of 1. The data points for each day are multiplied by their factors and sum totaled. This sum total is divided by the sum total of the factor weights (34+33+32+...1).

The Weighted Moving Average formula is:
WMA = Σ (factor x price) / Σ (factors).

A weighted moving average is very close to an exponential moving average. Figure 5-5 illustrates daily price action on J.P. Morgan (JPM). The dotted line is the weighted moving average (n=34) and the solid line is the exponential moving average (n=34).

Is there a connection between the use of averages and the use of Gann's swing lines? Figure 5-6 addresses this question. Early September 2022

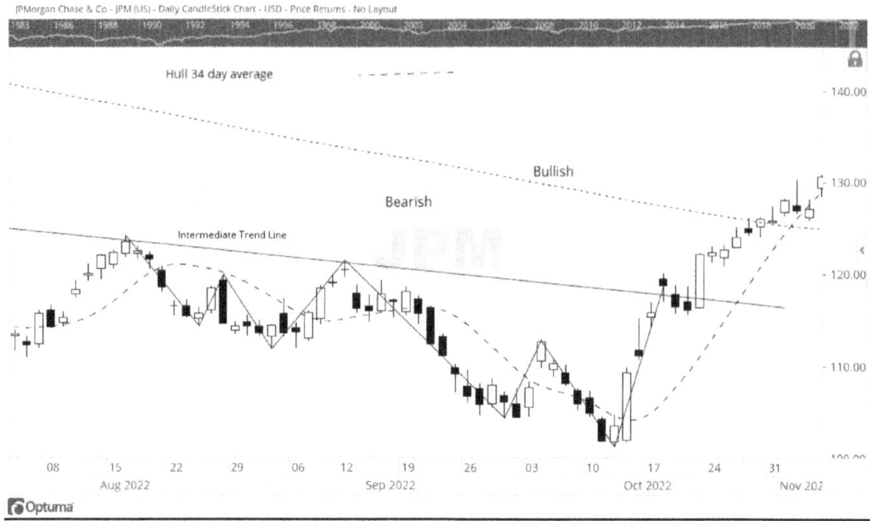

Figure 5-7

J.P. Morgan (JPM) with Hull average and swings

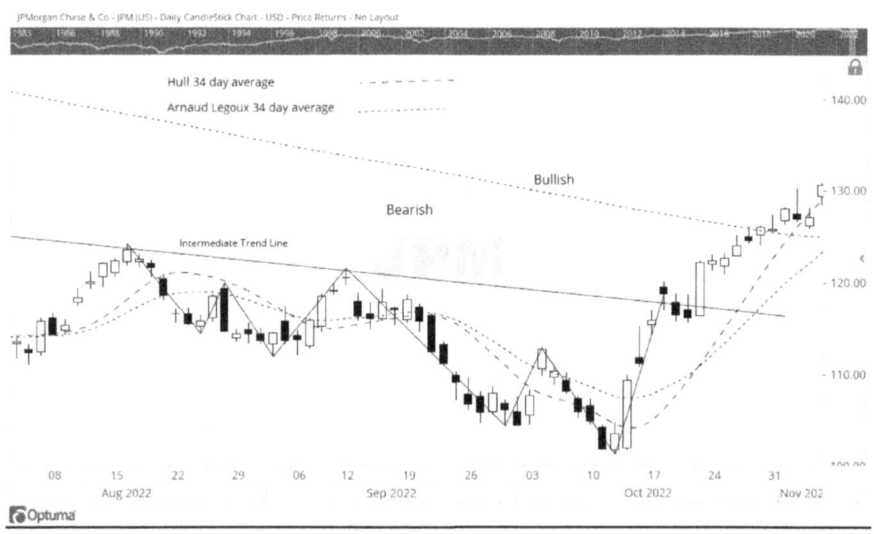

Figure 5-8

J.P. Morgan with Hull, and Arnaud Legoux averages

shows how price moved above a prior swing peak. A trader watching this development would have been cognizant that the major and intermediate trends were both bearish, hence no substantial gains could be expected from a trade. Nevertheless, the buy signal came as price took out the prior peak and as price crossed through the Wilder 34-day average. The price reversed once it hit the intermediate trend line. In October 2022, a similar situation presented itself. As price crossed through both the 34-day exponential moving average and the 34-day Wilder average, price moved above the prior peak, creating a buy signal.

The Hull Weighted Moving Average

The *Hull Weighted Moving Average* was created in 2005 by trader Dennis Hull. The Hull approach starts with identifying a period (n) for which a moving average is desired. A weighted moving average (WMA) is then calculated for the period n and for a period equal to $n/2$.

The difference between these two values is divided by the square root of n.

The Hull Moving Average formula is:
Hull WMA = Σ(2 x WMA for n/2 periods – WMA for n periods) / $\sqrt{n}$

In the case of a 34-day Hull Moving Average being applied to a chart, the mathematics would entail calculating a WMA for n=17 and also for n=34 days. The value of 2 x the 17-day WMA minus the 34-day WMA would be determined. This value would be divided by $\sqrt{n}$ = $\sqrt{34}$ = 5.83.

Figure 5-7 illustrates the J.P. Morgan price chart with the Hull 34-day average. Comparing Figure 5-7 to Figure 5-6 shows that the Hull average is more sensitive to price movement. In both September and October 2022, price crossed above the Hull average before crossing above the prior peak levels. The Hull average can be thought of as an early warning system that alerts traders to the possibility of a buy signal being developed.

Arnaud Legoux Moving Average

The *Arnaud Legoux Moving Average* was created in 2009 by traders Arnaud Legoux and Dimitrios Kouzis Loukas. Their goal was to create a smoother average than the Hull moving average.

The Arnaud Legoux moving average (ALMA) formula is:
$$ALMA = 1/Norm \ \Sigma \ data \ point(i) \ x \ e \ -(i-offset2)/\sigma^2 \ ;$$
where the summation occurs across the desired number of data points.

In this equation, the input data is fitted to a normal Gaussian distribution. The offset factor is normally taken as 0.85. The standard deviation (σ) is taken to be 6 standard deviations.

As Figure 5-8 illustrates, the *Arnaud Legoux Moving Average (ALMA)* is very close to the Hull moving average. Whether it is smoother than the Hull Average remains open to debate.

To Sum Up

The various software platforms traders use contain more moving average formulations than the ones I have presented in this chapter. The information presented in this chapter illustrates the mathematical construction of moving averages. This chapter further illustrates that some moving averages differ slightly from each other, while others differ markedly. A trader or investor should examine different n values for different types of moving averages, especially in the context of Gann swing highs and lows.

CHAPTER 6
MOVING AVERAGES AND THE TREND

The rudimentary computing power unleashed in the late 1980s led traders with mathematical and programming talent to start looking beyond just moving averages. Algorithms were developed that could mathematically smooth a moving average. Programs were written to calculate a signal line from price data. Technical chart indicators were then developed in which the action of a nuanced, smoothed average relative to a signal line acted as a trend-trading decision-making tool.

Know Sure Thing (KST) Indicator

The *Know Sure Thing* indicator was developed by trader Martin Pring in the early 1990s. This indicator utilizes the concept of rate of change. For example, on day 1 the closing value of a price bar is $5. The very next price bar in succession on day 2 comes in with a closing value of $6. The rate of change between day 1 and day 2 is calculated as ($6-$5)/($5) = 20%. The KST indicator also focuses on the concept of *smoothing*. Mathematically, if a series of moving average data points is itself averaged, that series of data points is

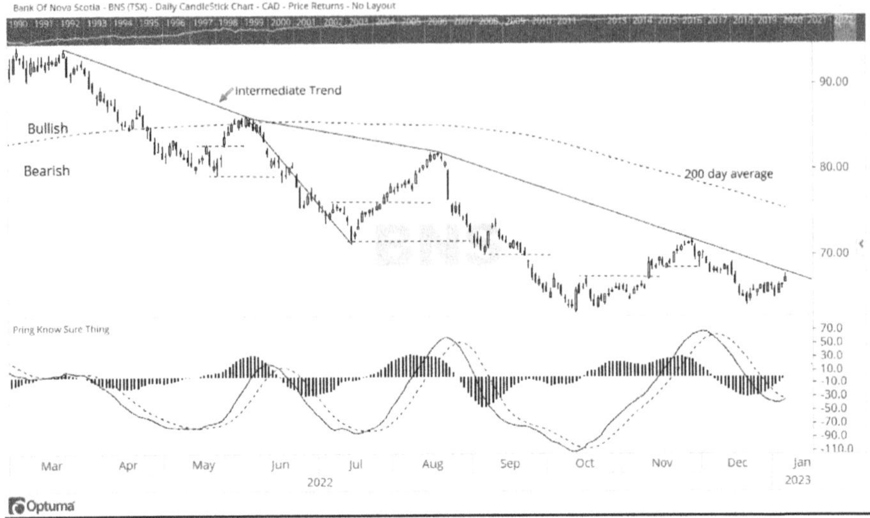

Figure 6-1

Scotiabank (BNS) daily chart with KST Indicator

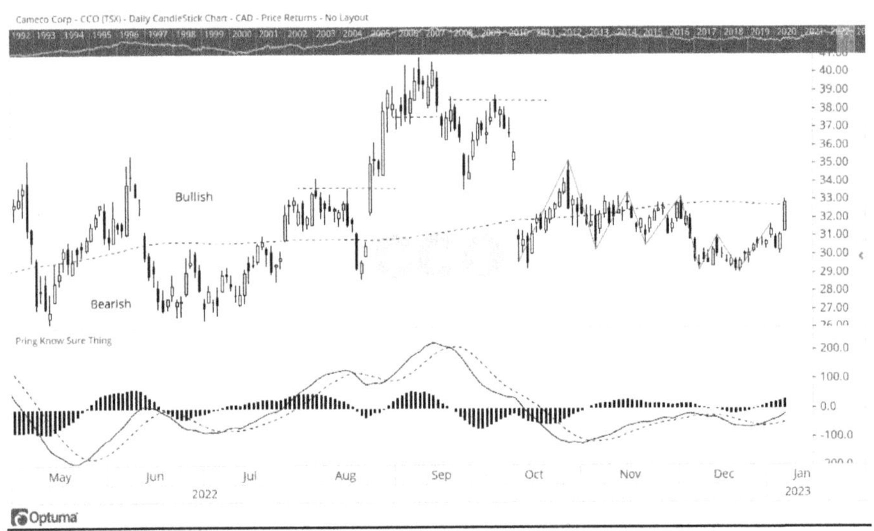

Figure 6-2

Cameco (CCO) daily Chart with KST indicator

said to have been *smoothed*. The KST indicator further utilizes a *signal line* which is a short-term moving average of the final calculated KST values.

The KST indicator is dependent on four rate of change (ROC) indicators, namely: the 10, 15, 20, and 30 day periods.

$$\text{The ROC formula is:}$$
$$ROC = [(\text{close p} - \text{close p-n})/(\text{close p-n})] \times 100;$$
$$\text{where } p \text{ is the current day and } n \text{ is the period}$$
$$(10,15,20,30) \text{ being considered.}$$

The ROC data for the 10, 15, and 20-day periods is smoothed by way of a 10-period moving average. The ROC data for the 30-day period is smoothed by way of a 15-period simple average.

The averaged ROC smoothed numbers are given weightings; 1, 2, 3 and 4 respectively.

An overall weighted figure is then calculated. The KST indicator is plotted on a vertical scale of +100 to -100. A 9-period average of KST values is then calculated to act as a signal line.

Figure 6-1 illustrates the daily price movements of Canadian financial institution ScotiaBank which trades on both Toronto and New York under the ticker BNS. The intermediate trend on BNS shifted to bearish in Q1 of 2022 when central bankers started raising interest rates. Shortly afterwards, the major trend shifted to bearish as well. The bearish intermediate pattern of a series of lower price tops has been illustrated with a descending solid line. The lower pane of the chart displays the Know Sure Thing (KST) Indicator.

Between May and December 2022, the declining price of BNS shares presented long buyers and short sellers alike with several opportunities. In May 2022, it was apparent that share price had been steadily declining since March. But, then the KST indicator line (solid) crossed over the signal line (dashed). A trader looking for a buying opportunity could have taken a long position at this KST crossover. To remove some of the risk from the trade, a more cautious approach would have been to use the Gann Prior Peak swing method. In fact, a couple days after the KST crossover, price surpassed the prior peak. Not a lot of profit would have resulted on the trade, but a small gain would have been recorded nonetheless. The reason for this tepid outcome is despite the KST buy signal, BNS was in a bearish major and bearish intermediate trend.

In June, as price fell to beneath a prior valley swing low point, the KST indicator line (solid) crossed over the signal line (dashed) to confirm the validity of the short selling strategy. In July, the KST indictor exhibited a positive crossover again, offering a trader an opportunity to take a long position. A more prudent approach would have involved waiting for price to cross above a previous swing peak, which it did several trading sessions later.

In late August, the KST indicator exhibited a crossover again. This was an invitation for a short seller to initiate a trade. A short seller needing additional confirmation of price weakness could have waited for price to fall below the prior swing low, which it did four trading sessions later. But, no sooner had price taken out the prior swing low than a small rally tried to gain traction. The KST indicator did not respond to this brief flurry of price action. The KST indicator remained negative with the indicator line below the signal line. Price eventually resumed its downward move.

In October, the KST indicator exhibited a positive crossover. A trader could have taken a long position at this point, or perhaps waited for price to surpass a prior peak. Either way, a small gain would have been realized on a trade. Small because the overall price trends (intermediate and major) were both bearish.

In early December, the KST indicator exhibited a bearish crossover. This aligned with price falling beneath a prior swing valley low.

This example of Bank of Nova Scotia (BNS) shares shows that the KST indicator can be used as a trade-entry decision-making tool. This example further illustrates that to remove at least a small amount of risk from a trade, the KST indicator can be used with the Gann Prior Peak swing methodology.

To illustrate another example of the KST indicator, consider the daily price action of Canadian uranium miner Cameco. Figure 6-2 illustrates price action on Cameco shares (TSX:CCO) for the last half of 2022.

In July 2022, the major trend on Cameco shifted to bullish. As price crossed above the 200-day average, the KST indicator had already crossed over positive to create a buy signal. A trader strictly following the KST indicator would have already been long of Cameco shares, but would have been experiencing some volatility. Once above the 200-day average, price action tried to press higher in August, but could not. After several sessions of sideways behavior, the KST indicator started to curl over. A trader observing this likely would have placed a stop loss order for protection. A couple sessions later, the KST indicator crossed over negative and price fell down below the 200-day average. Why did price struggle at this time? The answer is that price has risen to retrace Fibonacci 78.6% of the price decline in the month of June. Fibonacci retracements of 78.6% very often represent an exhaustion point where price will take a pause. The pause in this case saw price retrace Fibonacci 61.8% of its recent move upwards.

With this 61.8% retracement complete, a couple of trading sessions later, price moved above the 200-day average again. As price moved higher, it surpassed a prior peak. A couple sessions later, the KST indicator turned favorable again.

Figure 6-3

Tesla (TSLA) daily chart with KST indicator

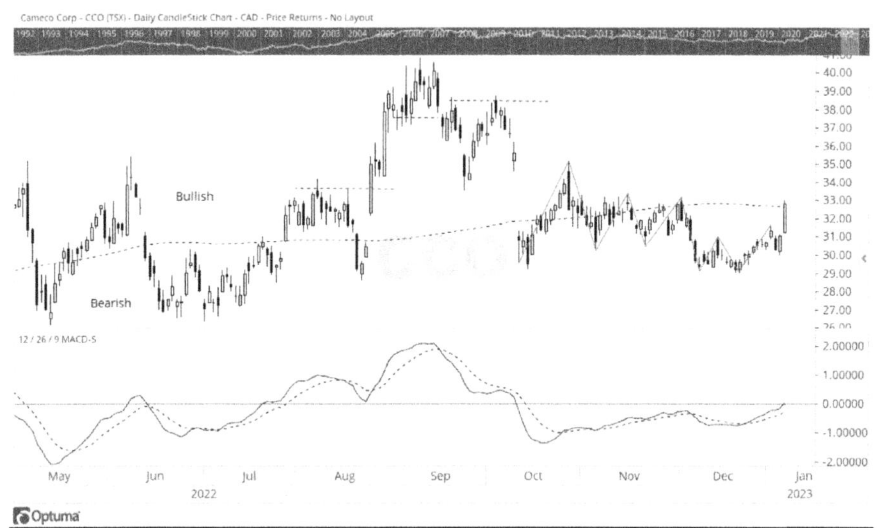

Figure 6-4

Cameco (CCO) daily Chart with MAC-D indicator

In mid-September, after hitting just over $40, price started to weaken.

Why? The answer is, price had retraced 100% of the downward move recorded in April and May. Price gapped lower and then proceeded to full the gap before turning weaker again. The KST indicator also crossed over bearish at this time too. Once more, price gapped lower and then proceeded to fill the gap. As the gap was being filled, the KST indicator did not signal the possibility of a long trade setup, nor did the Gann Prior Peak method. A trader paying attention to the KST indicator and to the Gann methodology would have been dissuaded from placing a buy order.

Towards the right side of Figure 6-2, during November and part of December, price action chopped back and forth with no trade setup being suggested by the Gann swing approach. The KST indicator was, however, favorable. A trader able to withstand volatility could possibly have engaged in some short-term activity. By January 9, 2023, a swing prior peak trade had presented itself again—the KST indicator was again signaling its approval.

As another example of the KST indicator interacting with the Prior Peak method and with Fibonacci, consider the daily price action of Tesla (TSLA) shown in Figure 6-3.

In January 2023, share price in Tesla had retraced Fibonacci 78.6% of a prior increase (mid-2020 through late 2021). This was a sign that a trend reversal could develop. In fact, it did and the KST indicator confirmed with a positive crossover. The intermediate trend line was next surpassed offering traders a further invitation to take a long position. By mid-February, price had retraced Fibonacci 48.6% of the late 2022 decline. The KST indicator was still favorable and the 200-day average was very close. The next logical target would have been 61.8% retracement, but in the waning days of February the KST indicator crossed negative and price began heading lower.

Figure 6-5

Scotiabank (BNS) daily Chart with MAC-D indicator

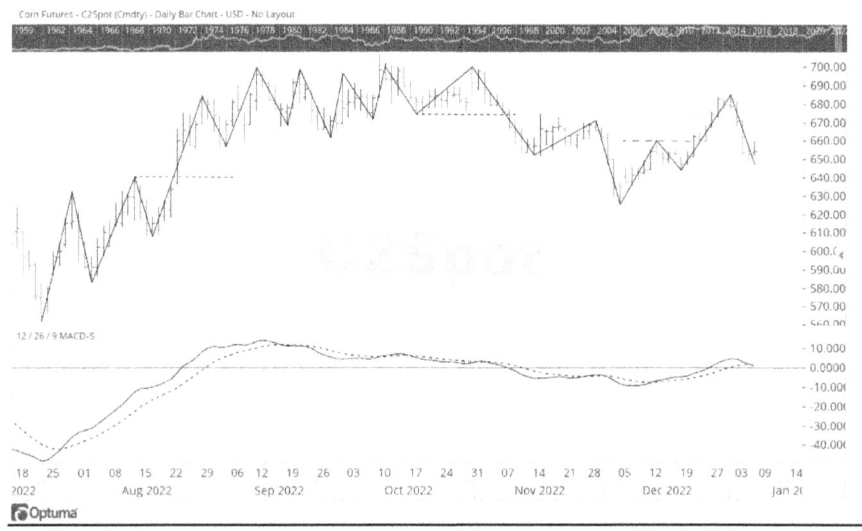

Figure 6-6

CBOT Corn futures with MAC-D indicator

MAC-D

In 1979, technical chartist Gerald Appel considered the relation between two exponential moving averages (EMA) of a series of price bars. He focused on 26 and 12-period exponential averages of closing prices (n=26 and n=12). He deemed the 26-period average to be slow moving versus the faster 12-period average. His computer algorithm calculated and plotted the difference between the two exponential averages. The algorithm plotted these differential data points; the resulting plot being called the *indicator line*. The algorithm then calculated a 9-period exponential moving average of these plotted data points to create the *signal line*.

Gerald Appel's indicator is now formally known as the *Moving Average Convergence Divergence* indicator and is abbreviated MAC-D.

The MAC-D formula is as follows:
MAC-D = [(12 day EMA – 26 day EMA)].

Crossovers of the indicator line above or below the signal line can be used to gauge changes in price trend. Moves of the MAC-D line above or below the zero line of the output plot can also be used to discern trend changes.

The chart in Figure 6-4 is the same as Figure 6-2, except the KST indicator has been replaced with the MAC-D indicator. The MAC-D indicator can be used alone or in conjunction with the Gann swing peaks and valleys technique.

Figure 6-5 is the same as Figure 6-1, except the KST indicator has been replaced by the MAC-D indicator. Once again, the MAC-D indicator is a valuable trading tool to help traders implement trades. However, to reduce volatility within the trade, it is better if the MAC-D was used in conjunction with the Gann Prior Peak methodology and with Fibonacci retracement mathematics.

The MAC-D indicator can also be used to examine the trend on commodity futures which tend to be more volatile than equity stocks. Figure 6-6 illustrates daily price action on continuous front month CBOT Corn futures.

At the left side of Figure 6-6, the MAC-D indicator exhibited a bullish crossover in July 2022. A trader taking a long position and strictly following the MAC-D would have been initially thrashed around by the volatility. A trader taking a long position in August when price surpassed a prior peak would have experienced somewhat less volatility as price moved higher.

In September 2022, price began to fluctuate in a broad sideways pattern with the prior peak methodology yielding no new trade signals. Why? The answer is, price was now pressing up against a Fibonacci 48.6% retracement of the decline from April through July 2022. With price unable to surpass the Fibonacci 48.6% level, the MAC-D soon crossed over bearish. Price then see-sawed lower into December.

By early December 2022, price had retraced Fibonacci 48.6% of the July through October advance. The MAC-D crossed over bullish, offering traders a signal to perhaps take along position in Corn futures. A more prudent approach would have been to wait until price surpassed the prior peak. While the MAC-D is adept at identifying trend shifts, to reduce volatility within the trade, it is better if the MAC-D was used in conjunction with the Gann swing peaks and valleys technique and the Fibonacci retracement mathematics. This hold especially true for commodity futures which are inherently more volatile than equity stocks.

TRIX

TRIX is an acronym for the triple exponential average, created in the early 1980s by Jack Hutson (who at the time was an editor with *Technical Analysis of Stocks and Commodities* magazine).

TRIX is very similar to the MAC-D indicator. There are four mathematical steps involved in the TRIX calculation:

1)   a 15-period Exponential Moving Average (EMA) of closing price is calculated

2)   a 15-period EMA of the data in step 1 is calculated

3)   a 15-period EMA of the data in step 2 is calculated

4)   a 1-period percentage change of the data points calculated in step 3 is plotted

5)   a 9-period simple average signal line is calculated from the data points in step 4.

Figure 6-7 illustrates share price action of pipeline operator Enbridge. Shares trade in Toronto and New York under the ticker ENB. Enbridge is a significant owner and operator of oil and natural gas pipelines across North America. The major trend on ENB turned bullish in March 2020. At the end of August 2022, the 200-day average was violated and several days later the pattern of higher cyclic lows was also breached. The trend on Enbridge then entered bearish territory. An attempt at crossing above the 200-day average was made in November 2022, but price failed to get into bullish territory.

The ENB chart in Figure 6-7 has further been fitted with the TRIX indicator. In July 2022, the TRIX indicator crossed over bullish. A trader taking a long position on the basis of this crossover would have encountered some volatile headwinds. Several trading session later, price surpassed the previous swing peak to confirm the bullish move.

In late August, price began receding from the $57 level. The TRIX indicator exhibited a bearish crossover. The crossover aligned neatly with price falling beneath a prior swing peak. Moreover, this price level was just slightly more than a Fibonacci 78.6% retracement of the increase from

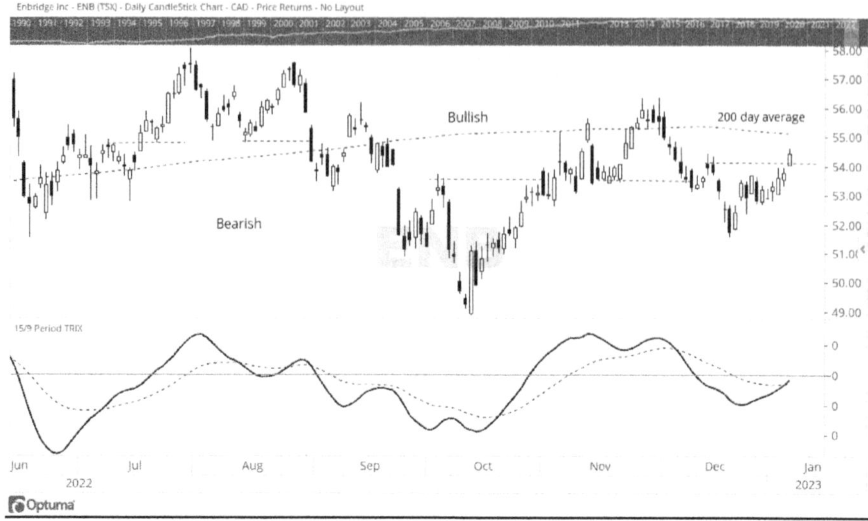

Figure 6-7

Enbridge (ENB) daily Chart with TRIX indicator

Figure 6-8

Silver futures (continuous front month) daily chart with TRIX

December 2021 through early June 2022. As well, the $57 level was a Fibonacci 78.6% retracement of the swift decline in June 2022.

In October, the TRIX indicator exhibited a bullish crossover. A trader taking a long position around the $51 level was rewarded with higher prices. A trader waiting for a confirming trade-entry invitation would have bought shares when price surpassed a prior swing peak at $53 to confirm the bullish trend. Price pressed higher into early December before running out of momentum. Why? The answer is price at the $56 level had retraced Fibonacci 78.6% of the decline from August through October. More recently, at the right side of the chart, the TRIX indicator started to cross bullish in early January 2023 just as price surpassed a prior swing peak. This turn of trend also aligned to price having retraced Fibonacci 61.8% of the decline from November through mid-December.

The TRIX indicator is a valuable tool for identifying trend changes. Used on its own, a trade implemented can turn out to be more volatile than expected. Some of this volatility can be removed from the trade by also relying on the Gann prior swing peaks and valleys technique and on Fibonacci retracement mathematics.

As an example of the TRIX indicator being used to trade a commodity futures contract, consider the case of Silver futures as illustrated in Figure 6-8.

Figure 6-8 has been fitted with horizontal dashed lines indicating various Fibonacci retracement levels of the price decline from March through August 2022. In September 2022, the TRIX indicator crossed positive to create a buying signal. A trader acting on this signal alone would have taken a long position on Silver just as price was about to hit the Fibonacci 23.6% retracement level and begin a decline. Most certainly, this would have been a losing trade. The TRIX indicator stayed positive into mid-October. In early October, price surpassed a prior swing peak at the $20 level. A trader acting on this development and noting that TRIX was positive could have realized the better part of a $1 per ounce move higher ($5000 per contract) on Silver. Price then ran out of momentum at the Fibonacci 38.2% retracement level. This flagging momentum was confirmed as TRIX recorded a negative crossover.

In early November, the TRIX indicator provided another positive crossover. A trader buying Silver futures at this crossover indication was certainly running the risk of price behaving in a volatile fashion. In this case, the volatility was low and price soon worked its way higher. A trader noting the positive TRIX indicator and seeking further confirmation of a buy signal could have waited for price to surpass the prior swing high at the $21 per ounce level. By the time price got just over $22, momentum was waning. This was the Fibonacci 68.2% retracement of the decline from March through August 2022.

In early December, momentum was starting to firm up. As price surpassed the prior swing peak and got over the 200-day average, the major trend turned bullish. A trader entering a Silver trade could have realized the better part of a $2 per ounce move higher. Momentum started to soften and price lapsed into a sideways consolidation pattern. Why? This price level was the Fibonacci 78.6% retracement of the decline from March through August 2022. In late December, the TRIX indicator turned negative and at this time of writing in mid-February 2023 remains negative.

This example of Silver shows that the TRIX indicator is not always accurate. It ideally should be used in conjunction with prior swing peaks and with Fibonacci mathematics.

To Sum Up

TRIX, MAC-D, and the KST are three powerful indicators all mathematically based on the use of moving averages. If used alone, the trader can sometimes end up enduring unwanted volatility and trade losses. When used in collaboration with price surpassing prior peaks and valleys and Fibonacci mathematics, the timing of when the trade is implemented changes and some of the trade volatility will be eliminated.

93

94

CHAPTER 7
OSCILLATORS AND THE TREND

Instead of just focusing on averages and signal lines to create chart indicators, traders and programmers also developed indicators based on a comparison of absolute prices relative to a price range over a recently defined period of *n* price bars.

For example, consider taking price data over a period of n=14 days. Express the price data points as a percentage of the highest price observed over those past n=14 days. If this percentage value is seen to be rising, price momentum (the trend) is deemed to be bullish. As this calculated percentage value begins to slow, an alert trader will start to anticipate a possible bearish price trend manifesting.

If these calculated percentage values are plotted on a chart whose vertical scale has an upper (positive) and lower (negative) boundary, along with a mid-scale zero-line, the plot is termed an *oscillator*. If the data input into the oscillator function calculations is random, the oscillator is termed a *stochastic oscillator*. Price data of stocks, commodity futures, ETFs, and indices are *random signals*. That is, the price on a given day is not a guaranteed reflection of price the day before or the day after.

Interpreting stochastic oscillators in a stand-alone manner is difficult. Stochastic oscillators exhibiting values near their upper boundary are termed *overbought* and can often signal an approaching change of trend from bullish to bearish. However, this is not a certainty in all cases. Stochastic oscillators exhibiting values near their lower boundary are termed *oversold* and can be a sign of a pending bullish trend formation. However, this is also not a certainty. A stochastic oscillator moving from near its lower boundary up and through the zero line can be indicative of a trend change. Likewise, a trend change can develop as a stochastic oscillator moves from near its upper boundary down through the zero line. In many cases, an oscillator moving above its upper boundary line can create a buy signal. A move from above the upper bound to below the upper bound can create a sell signal.

This chapter focuses on the mathematics behind a variety of stochastic oscillators.

Percent Price Oscillator

As a follow-up to the MAC-D indicator, Gerald Appel created what he called the Percent Price Oscillator (PPO). He based this oscillator function on the difference between two exponential moving averages; the 12-day and 26-day. These are the same moving averages that he used in creating the MAC-D indicator. Instead of plotting this difference, he expressed this difference as a fraction of the 26-day average. The formula he crafted is:

PPO = [(12 day EMA − 26 day EMA) / 26 day EMA] x 100.

A plot of the PPO indicator will range from a scale of minus values to plus values. Once at least 9 data points have been obtained, a 9-day exponential moving average (EMA) is calculated and added to the plot as a signal line.

When the chart in Figure 7-1 was generated, the major trend on Disney was bearish with prices beneath the 200-day average. The intermediate trend was also bearish as evidenced by a series of lower price tops. The company's diversification into the overcrowded media streaming sector had not gone well, which had emboldened the bearish trend.

When the chart in Figure 7-1 was generated, the major trend on Disney was bearish with prices beneath the 200-day average. The intermediate trend was also bearish as evidenced by a series of lower price tops. The company's diversification into the overcrowded media streaming sector has not gone well, which has emboldened the bearish trend.

Despite the bearish trends, an aggressive trader could have executed a series of long trades between May and December 2022. In June, the PPO exhibited a bullish crossover. A trader acting on this signal would have been met with some volatility. Waiting until mid-July when price surpassed the prior swing high would have helped sidestep some of this volatility. Price rallied to touch the intermediate trend line. A trader seeing that price was struggling to penetrate the trendline likely would have exited the trade. The PPO displaying a bearish crossover would have certainly meant an exit from the trade. This failure of price to surpass the intermediate trend line came at a Fibonacci 61.8% retracement of the price decline from April through mid-July 2022.

In October, the PPO exhibited a positive crossover. This came as price had just completed a 100% retracement of the July through August price increase. Share price rallied, touched the intermediate trend line, and retreated. The PPO recorded a negative crossover. This failure of price to press higher came at a Fibonacci 48.6% retracement of the August through October decline.

In November, the PPO again signaled a possible trade entry opportunity.

Figure 7-1

Walt Disney Co. (DIS) with Percent Price Oscillator (PPO)

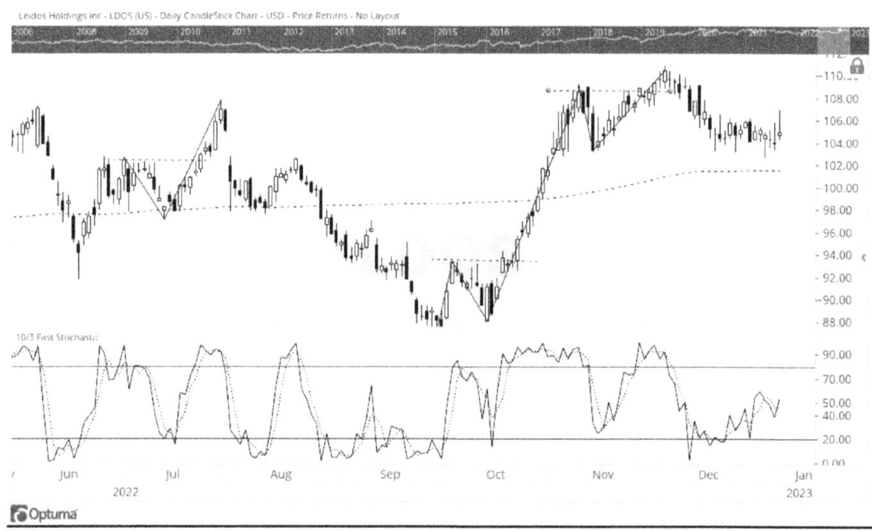

Figure 7-2

LDOS Holdings (LDOS) daily chart with Fast Stochastic

Price surpassing a small prior peak added confirmation of the trade opportunity. However, a trader acting on these signals would have been

met with price action that drifted sideways-to-lower into mid-December. The PPO also drifted sideways indicating a lack of enthusiasm on the part of buyers. The feature that was preventing price from advancing was overhead resistance at the Fibonacci 61.8% retracement level of November price decline.

Early January 2023 brought another PPO bullish signal. The fundamental news that stimulated investors was the return of the former CEO to try to fix the problems created by the company's misadventure into media streaming. In mid-January 2023, price surpassed a prior peak, adding confirmation to the bullish trade bias. In mid-February, price lost momentum and the PPO indicator crossed over negative. Why? Price had retraced Fibonacci 78.6% of the overall August to December 2022 decline.

The PPO indicator is a valuable tool for traders and investors to embrace. Ideally it should be used in collaboration with price surpassing prior peaks and valleys and with Fibonacci mathematics.

Fast Stochastic Oscillator

The *Fast Stochastic Oscillator* was derived in 1948 by Chicago-based stock and commodity trader Ralph Dystant. In the mid-1940s, Mr. Dystant started a trading school called *Investment Educators*. The goal of the school was to teach people stock trading and charting techniques. His trading school eventually expanded in the 1950s to include commodity futures trading. Other staff soon joined the school, among them, the acclaimed chartist George Lane.

The Fast Stochastic Oscillator is based on both the lowest price and highest price over a recent span of n price bars or candlesticks. The closing price on a given day relative to these reference points creates a stochastic statistical measure. In many software platforms, this stochastic measure is called %K.

The following formula shows how %K is calculated.
%K = 100 * [(Closing price -Ln)/(Hn-Ln)];
where Ln is the lowest price in the past n periods,
Hn is the highest price in the past n periods,
and Closing Price is the close of the current day's trading session.

Dystant, and his students went on to create a nuance of the %K value.

They created a short-term function; the %D function:
%D = 100 * [(Closing price -L3)/(H3-L3)];
where L3 is the lowest price in the past 3 periods,
H3 is the highest price in the past 3 periods,
and Closing Price is the close of the current day's trading session.

Taken together, %K and %D, when plotted comprise the Fast Stochastic. Dystant and his team said that a Fast Stochastic value of 20 is generally representative of a stock, commodity or index that is oversold and ready for a turn bullish. They regarded a value of 80 to be overbought and ready to turn bearish.

If this was the general observation in the late 1940s, today's faster moving markets require a slight adjustment in how the Fast Stochastic can be interpreted. My observations across a wide variety of stocks suggests that the 80 level on the Stochastic plot can *often* (not exclusively) represent the point at which a buying decision is made.

To illustrate, the chart of Leidos Holdings (LDOS) in Figure 7-2 has been fitted with the Fast Stochastic in the lower pane. The timeframe covered by this chart is from mid-2022 to February 2023. Leidos Holdings is a major player in the artificial intelligence field. The solid line is the %K, the dashed line is the %D. The solid line crossing above the dashed line suggests a bullish tone to price action. The default settings for the Fast Stochastic are 10 days for the %K and 3 days for the %D. The Fast Stochastic display pane has also been fitted with two horizontal lines; a sell line and a buy line. The sell line is the lower of the two lines at the 20 level. The buy line is the higher of the two lines at the 80 level.

In June 2022, LDOS share price had been declining from the $107 level. Along the way, the Fast Stochastic fell beneath the 20 level (the Sell Line). The temptation would have been to buy the stock on the assumption that price was oversold and due for a recovery. There is an adage that traders often express: *an oversold stock can remain oversold longer than a person can remain solvent.* In other words, just because a stock chart indicator shows that the stock is oversold should not be reason enough to buy the stock.

In the case of LDOS, the Fast Stochastic bounced around beneath the 20 level (Sell line) for six trading sessions before finally moving above the 20 level (Sell line). Price had by now retraced Fibonacci 61.8% of the overall increase that occurred between February and April 2022. A trader buying LDOS shares as the Fast Stochastic moved above the 20 level would have enjoyed a profitable trade. To mitigate the risk of price action behaving in a volatile fashion, a trader could have waited for a few more days. On June 23, price action moved above the 200-day average. At the same time, the Fast Stochastic moved above the Buy line (the 80 level). A trader taking a long position at this juncture would still have enjoyed a gain on the trade.

Note in Figure 7-2 how the Fast Stochastic then moved above and below the 80 line as price struggled with overhead resistance at the $102 level. This was the Fibonacci 61.8% retracement of the early June decline. This resistance proved too much and by mid-July, price had faded to rest right atop the 200-day average. The Stochastic touched the 20 level and then recorded a favorable crossover. A trader buying LDOS at this point would have realized a profit on a trade. A slightly smaller profit would have been realized by a trader waiting for the Stochastic to get above the 80 level.

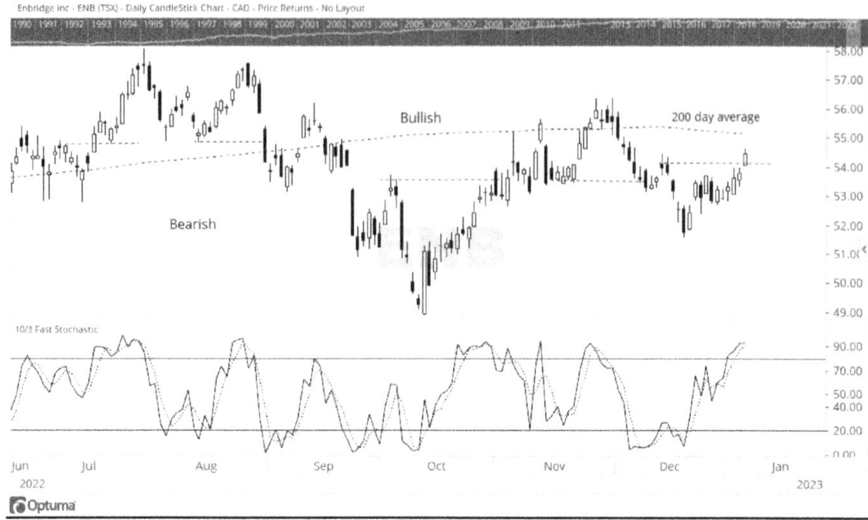

Figure 7-3

Enbridge (ENB) daily chart with Fast Stochastic

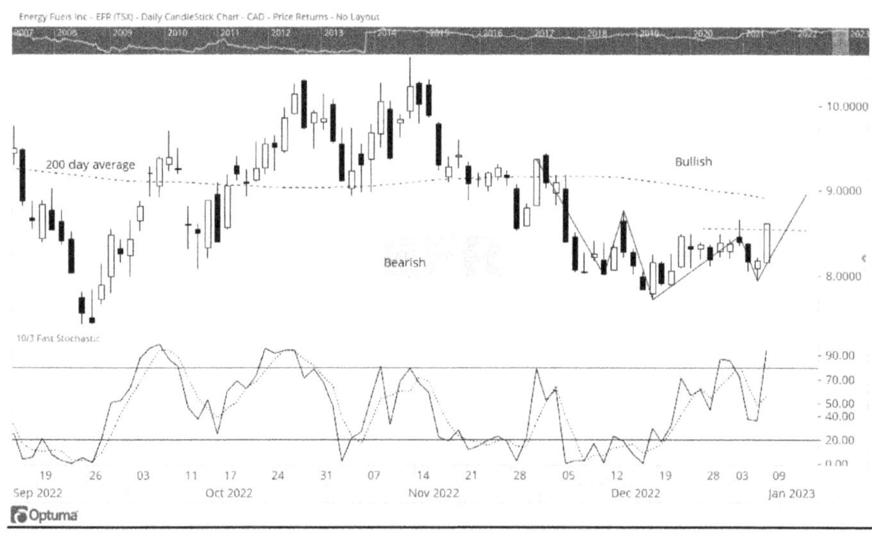

Figure 7-4

Energy Fuels (TSX:EFR) daily chart with Fast Stochastic

This occurred as price surpassed a prior swing high from late June. Price ran out of momentum at the $107 level which was also the Fibonacci 78.6% retracement of the April through June decline.

On August 1, price began to recede, the Fast Stochastic fell beneath the 80 level and price gapped downwards, coming to rest again atop the 200-day average. On August 11, the Fast Stochastic emerged from beneath the 20 level (Sell line). A trader taking a long position would have done so in hopes of the price gap being filled. On August 16, the Fast Stochastic again moved above the 80 mark. On August 22, the Stochastic rolled over and fell beneath the 80 level. The gap would not be filled. It was time to exit the trade.

In early October, LDOS price had retraced 78.6% of the overall advance that had occurred between February and April 2022. The Stochastic then moved above the lower bound (20 level) to offer a buy signal. Price moved higher along with the Stochastic. The Stochastic then failed to surpass the 80- level upper bound. Price quickly reversed on itself and fell lower. This is a good example to illustrate my earlier observation that sometimes it is prudent to wait for the Stochastic to surpass the upper bound (80 level).

On October 18, recovering price surpassed a prior peak and the Fast Stochastic moved above the 80 level (Buy line). A trader taking a long position at this signal would have been amply rewarded with a $15 per share move. A trader would have known to exit the trade and take profit when the Fast Stochastic eased beneath the 80 level on November 9. A similar situation presented itself on November 25 as price surpassed a prior swing high and the Fast Stochastic moved above 80. December 5 saw the Fast Stochastic fall beneath the 80 level, signaling an end to the trade.

On January 20, the Stochastic moved above the 20 level, suggesting a buying opportunity at the $95 level. Price at that point had declined Fibonacci 61.8% of the October to late December 2022 price gain. Analysts

Figure 7-5

Silver futures (continuous front month) with Fast Stochastic

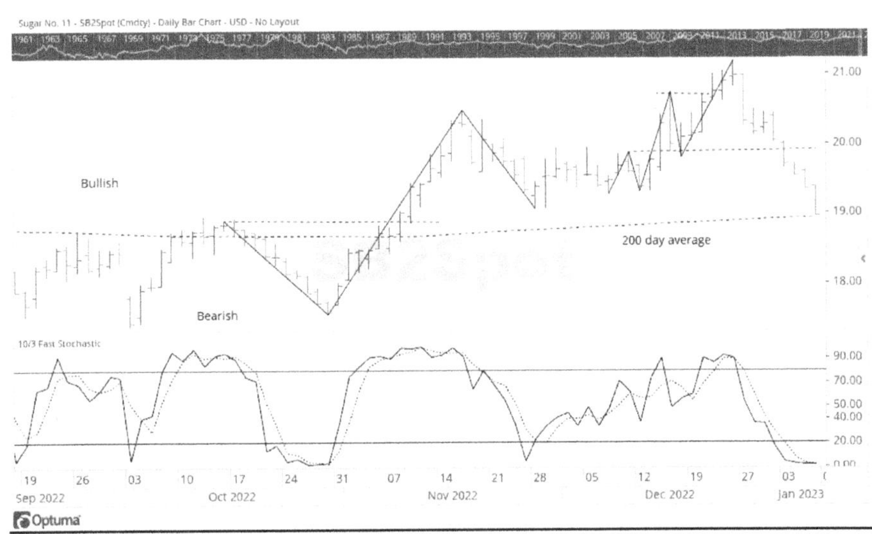

Figure 7-6

Sugar futures (front month) daily chart with Fast Stochastic

were suggesting that the share price could soon hit the $150 level. Price went on to rally to the $102 level, a Fibonacci 48.6% retracement of the December 2022 to late January 2023 decline. Suddenly in mid-February price ran out of momentum. The Company Q4 earnings release explained the flagging momentum. While earnings were solid, the Company reminded shareholders that its major customer is the US government and that the government is tightening up on spending programs. This news quickly sank share prices by $4 per share, taking the stochastic beneath the 80 level. The wait for a new buy signal at some point in the future started anew.

The Fast Stochastic indicator appears to be the reason Mr. Dystant and his group of students reportedly made so much money trading the markets. However, in today's fast markets, this indicator should be used in conjunction with Fibonacci mathematics and prior swing peak strategies.

Figure 7-3 is a daily chart of pipeline operator Enbridge (ENB). The price chart has been fitted with the Fast Stochastic in the lower pane. The timeframe covered by the chart is from July 2022 to early January 2023. Along the way, on four occasions, the Fast Stochastic moved above the 80 level (Buy line). Taking a long position as the Fast Stochastic moved above the upper boundary yielded favorable results at each event. At the far right of the chart, the upper bound was surpassed on January 3, 2023. On January 6, price surpassed a prior swing peak.

Figure 7-4 is a daily chart of uranium refiner and rare earth metals producer Energy Fuels (TSX:EFR). Although the stock trades on the Toronto Exchange, its processing plant is situated in Blanding, Utah. In 2023, it will start advancing a rare earth mineral sands project in Brazil. The price chart has been fitted with the Fast Stochastic in the lower pane. The timeframe covered by the chart is from September 2022 to early January 2023. In October, on two occasions the Fast Stochastic moved above its upper boundary line. Both moves also aligned to price surpassing prior peaks. At the far right side of the chart, price surpassed a prior swing high

($8.50) as Stochastic moved above the 80 level. The resulting move took share price to $10.30. Momentum than quickly faded because this rally had retraced 100% of the November-December 2022 decline.

Figure 7-5 illustrates daily price action on the continuous front month Silver futures contract. The chart has been fitted with the Fast Stochastic. The timeframe covered by the chart is from October 2022 to January 2023.

Over the timeframe covered by this chart there were several moves of the Fast Stochastic above the upper boundary line. Three of these moves were associated with the price of Silver surpassing a prior swing peak. At the right side of the chart note that there were a couple efforts in December by the Fast Stochastic to surpass the upper bound Sell line (80 level). Price was unable to surpass a prior peak and the Fast Stochastic faded to a lower level. If Silver prices are to move higher in 2023, price will have to surpass $25 per ounce and the Fast Stochastic will have to confirm the move.

Figure 7-6 illustrates daily price action on Sugar futures (continuous front month chart). In the final months of 2022, there were three instances of the Fast Stochastic moving above its upper bound level. A trader taking a long position in Sugar futures as the Fast Stochastic moved from deeply oversold to above the lower bound (Sell line, 20 level) certainly would have been risking volatile trading conditions. But, as Figure 7-6 shows, these trades were rewarding. Waiting for the Stochastic to get above the upper bound line and for price to surpass a prior peak provided less volatility, but smaller trade gains. In early January 2023, Sugar prices retreated to rest atop the 200-day average. This price decline was a Fibonacci 61.8% retracement of the overall advance from late October through late December. At this time of writing, Sugar prices did move higher from their precarious perch atop the 200-day average. A trader taking a long position either as the Stochastic moved above the 20 level or as it moved above the 80 level would have been rewarded.

Slow Stochastic

The Slow Stochastic is a variation of the Fast Stochastic. In the Slow Stochastic, the %D is taken as being a 3-bar simple moving average of the %K function. The application of a 3-bar moving average serves to smooth out the oscillator function making decision making for traders easier.

To compare the Fast Stochastic to the Slow Stochastic, Figure 7-7 again illustrates the daily price action on Sugar futures. The lower pane on the chart has been fitted with the Slow Stochastic. Notice that the general profile of the Slow Stochastic plot is smoother than that of the Fast Stochastic. As with the Fast Stochastic, buying as the stochastic emerges from beneath the 20 level might entail volatility. Waiting until the stochastic is breaking above the upper bound (80 level) will involve less volatility. A more prudent approach is to use the Slow Stochastic in conjunction with Fibonacci retracements and the Gann prior peak strategy.

Williams % R

The *Williams % R indicator* is a stochastic function invented by trader and author Larry Williams.

The Williams %R indicator compares the current price to the range of the highest and lowest prices over a lookback period, usually n=14 days. The %R function is graphed using a vertical axis scale that runs from -100 to 0. When the %R moves up and through (or down and through) a selected level, the trend is deemed to be changing.

Figure 7-8 illustrates price action on US energy producer Devon Energy (DVN). The chart, which covers the timeframe August 2022 through January 2023, has been fitted with the Williams %R indicator with a 14-period setting. The major trend of Devon Energy was bullish for much of 2022, but slipped into bearish territory in December.

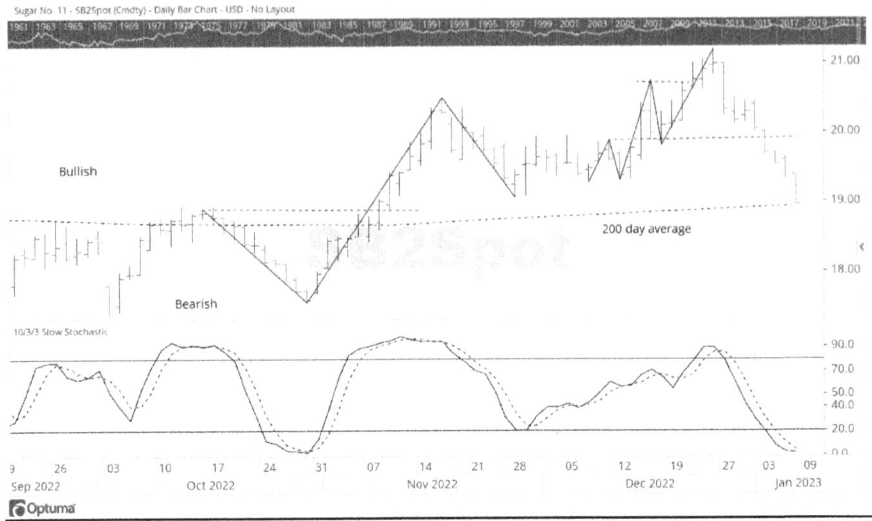

Figure 7-7

Sugar futures (front month) daily chart with Slow Stochastic

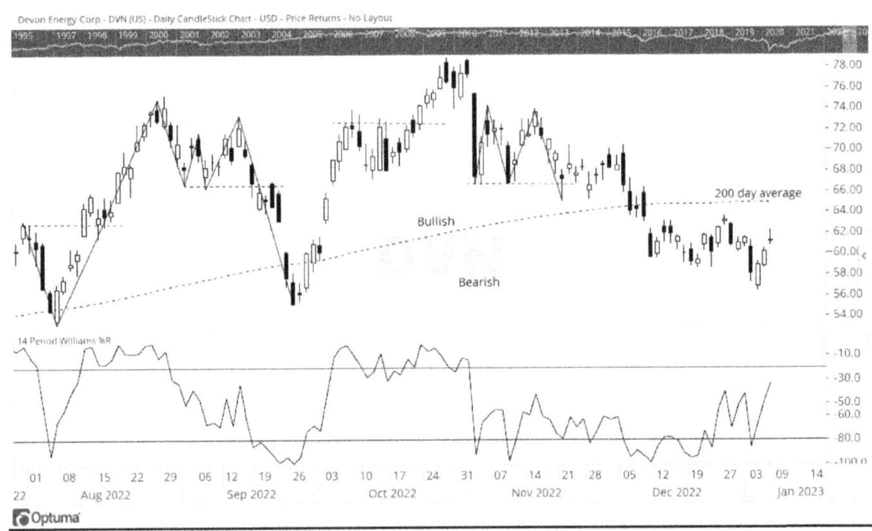

Figure 7-8

Devon Energy (DVN) daily chart with Williams %R

In August, share price surpassed a prior swing peak. The Williams %R at the same time moved above its upper bound level (-20). Share prices went on to move nearly $10 higher. Momentum stalled on August 29 as price reached the Fibonacci 78.6% retracement of the early June–early July price decline.

In September, prices began to fade. A short sell signal was provided when price moved beneath a prior swing valley (horizontal dashed line). At this selling indication, notice that the Williams %R dipped beneath its lower bound line (-80).

At the end of September, the Williams %R was trying to emerge from beneath the lower bound level (-80). Share price had also recorded a Fibonacci 78.6% retracement at this time. A trader buying DVN shares at this time would have realized a profitable trade. A trader waiting for the Williams %R to reach its upper bound (-20) would entered the trade just as price was filling the prior gap. The net result would have been a profitable trade.

In early November, price momentum stalled as price had retraced 100% of the early June–early July price decline. The Williams %R indicator dipped beneath its upper bound (-20) to signal that the trend was turning.

In early January 2023, the Williams %R indicator touched its lower bound (-80) and proceeded to turn higher. This occurred as price was completing a Fibonacci 78.6% retracement of the September-November 2022 advance.

This example of the Williams %R indicator applied to price action on Devon Energy suggests that the Williams %R indicator is one that traders and investors should consider using. However, in today's fast markets, this indicator should be used in conjunction with Fibonacci mathematics and prior swing peak strategies.

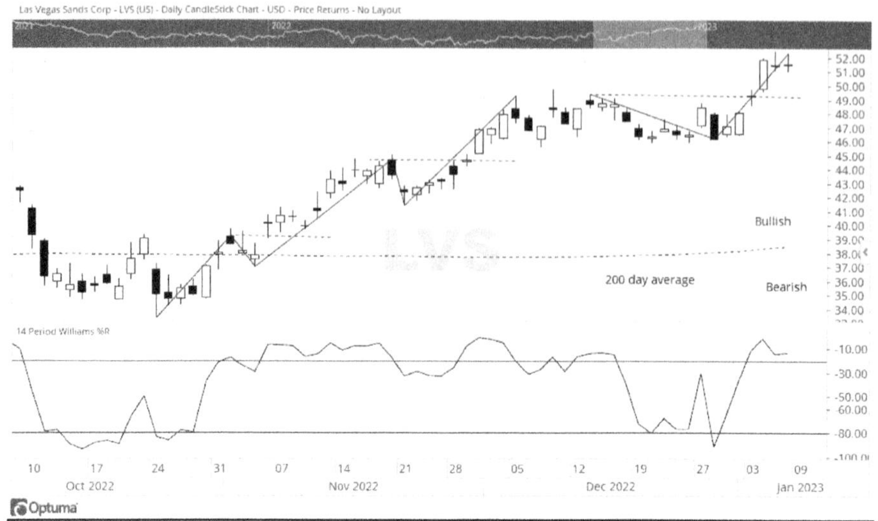

Figure 7-9

Las Vegas Sands (LSV) daily chart with Williams %R

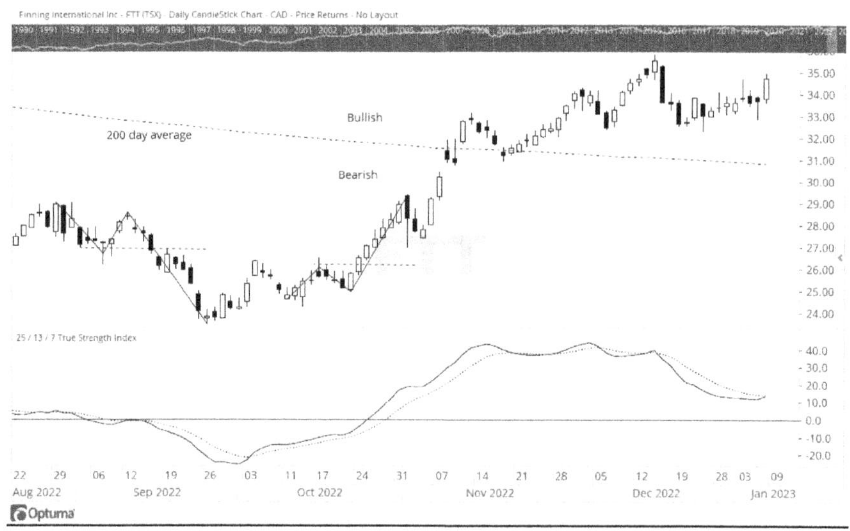

Figure 7-10

Finning International (TSX: FTT) daily chart with True Strength Index

Figure 7-9 illustrates price action on casino operator Las Vegas Sands (LSV). The chart has been fitted with the Williams %R indicator with a 14-period setting. The major trend on the stock shifted to bullish in November 2022 when China announced a relaxation of COVID lockdown rules. With the easing, residents could again travel to the island of Macau to gamble at the various LSV-owned properties on the island.

On November 4, price surpassed a prior swing peak to give a buy signal. The Williams %R surpassed its upper bound level to confirm the signal. On November 30, a similar buy signal occurred. Uncertainties over the COVID situation in China caused LSV share price to trend sideways in December after having retraced 48.6% of the overall March 2021 through May 2022 decline. As the COVID lockdown news clarified itself, price began its upward move. Price momentum stalled in late January 2023 at the $60 level and began to point lower. The Williams %R confirmed this development. Price had fully retraced Fibonacci 78.6% of the overall March 2021 through May 2022 decline.

True Strength Index

The True Strength Index was developed by trader William Blau in the early 1990s. Its mathematics employ a technique called double smoothing. The double smoothing calculations entail a three-step process.

> » First, the price change from one period to the next is calculated. This price differential can be based on the closing price, the high price, the low price, or an average between the daily high and low. Note that negative numbers could result from these price change calculations. This is why the True Strength function uses the absolute value of the price change.
> » Second, a 25-period exponential moving average (EMA) of the price data from step one is calculated. This is the first smoothing of the data.
> » Third, a 13-period EMA of the 25-period EMA data from step

two is calculated. This calculation of an average of an average is what imparts the double smoothing aspect to this indicator.

The calculation algorithm then repeats itself, this time using the absolute values of price changes. For example, if the price on one day is $10 and the price the next day is $9, the price change is -$1. The absolute value of this price change would be stated as +$1.

The same double smoothing EMA calculations are done to the absolute price data.

After these dual calculations, the double smoothed price change is divided by the absolute double smoothed price change. The result is multiplied by 100.

The algorithm further entails a signal line computed from a 7-day EMA of the calculated True Strength values.

When the True Strength Index crosses above the zero line, the short term trend is changing to bullish. If the True Strength Index crosses below the zero line, the short term trend is changing to bearish.

The daily chart of Finning International, a Canadian-headquartered global distributor of Caterpillar heavy equipment is presented in Figure 7-10. The True Strength Index has been fitted to bottom pane of the chart. Default settings of 25, 13, and 7 have been used.

In September 2022, share price fell beneath a prior swing valley. This signaled the possibility for a short selling opportunity. Moreover, this move signaled a resumption of a bearish trend. The True Strength Index provided confirmation when it slipped beneath the zero line. In late October, price moved above a prior swing peak to signal a buying opportunity. The True Strength Index moved above the zero line to provide confirmation that the trend was shifting.

In mid-January, the True Strength Index was still above the zero line. November and December provided two additional instances where price moved above a small prior swing peak. The key observation is that the True Strength Index did not gravitate back and forth across the zero line in response to these smaller individual moves. In this regard, the True Strength Index really does act as a "true" measure of the trend. As with some other indicators, a trader could also be watching for the True Strength indicator line to cross above the signal line as a prompt to take a long position. To reduce the volatility of the trade, waiting for a cross of the True Strength Index above the zero line in conjunction with price surpassing a prior peak is a prudent approach. The use of Fibonacci mathematics is also recommended.

Figure 7-11 illustrates daily price action on General Motors (GM). The chart has been fitted with the True Strength Index. In July 2022, share price surpassed a prior swing peak. The True Strength Index which was beneath the zero line, exhibited a bullish crossover. Price pressed a bit higher and then pulled back, creating a swing peak. As price moved above this swing peak four trading sessions later, the True Strength Index held above the zero line, maintaining the bullish signal.

In late September, price momentum began to fade as the Fibonacci 38.2% retracement level loomed on the horizon. Price declined, crossed beneath a prior swing valley point. The True Strength Index moved beneath the zero line in agreement.

In October, price decided to rally again. Price moving above a prior swing high signaled the bullish sentiment and the True Strength Index moved above the zero line to confirm. By December, price had started to fade after having struggled to get decisively above the 200-day average. Overhead resistance at the $41.50 level was a 100% retracement of the September-October decline. Price fell beneath a prior swing valley and beneath the 200-day average. The True Strength Index fell beneath the zero line. The trend had changed. In early January 2023, the True Strength Index

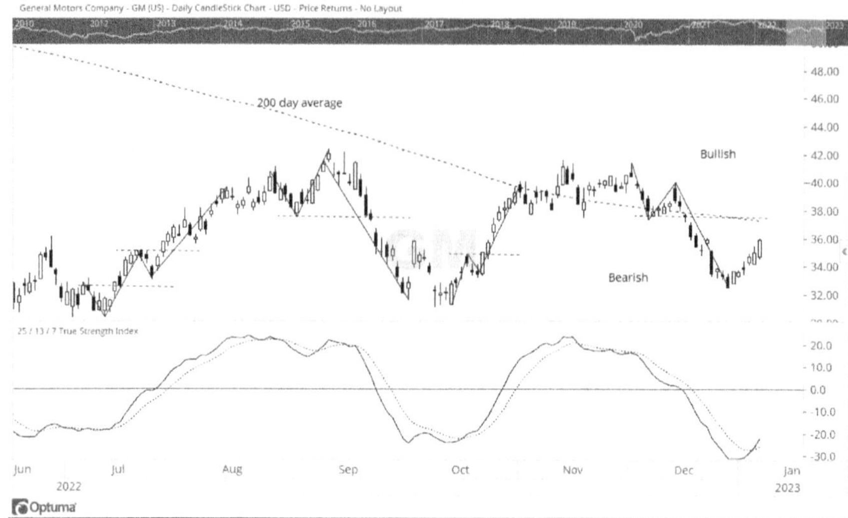

Figure 7-11

General Motors (GM) daily chart with True Strength Index

Figure 7-12

US Steel (X) daily chart with RSI

expressed a positive crossover. Price had declined a Fibonacci 78.6% of the October-November 2022 price gain. Although not shown in Figure 7-11, price advanced by a 61.8% retracement of the December drawdown. Price briefly retreated. As price started to firm up, the True Strength Index crossed above the zero line to provide a buy signal. Price then advanced by just over $7 over the ensuing two weeks.

Relative Strength Index

The *RSI Index*, an oscillator function, was developed by trader J. Welles Wilder in the late 1970s as a means of indicating the prevailing trend of a stock or commodity. There are two steps to its calculation.

In step one, data for n=14 price bars or candlesticks is examined. The daily gain or daily loss is noted for each period; the gains from the up days are averaged and the gains for the down days are averaged. Why Mr. Wilder focused on n=14 is not made clear in his writings.

In step two, the following formula is applied:

$$RS = \left[\frac{100 - 100}{1 + \left\{ \frac{\text{(sum of gains over past 14 periods/14)}}{\text{(sum of losses over past 14 periods /14)}} \right\}} \right]$$

In step three, the RS value from step two is smoothed
to generate the RSI value as follows:
$$RSI = (100 - (100/1 + RS)).$$

The chart in Figure 7-12 is that of steelmaker US Steel (NYSE: X). The timeframe for the chart is from October 2022 to early January 2023. The lower pane of the chart has been fitted with the 14-period RSI.

Figure 7-13

Amazon (AMZN) with Commodity Channel index

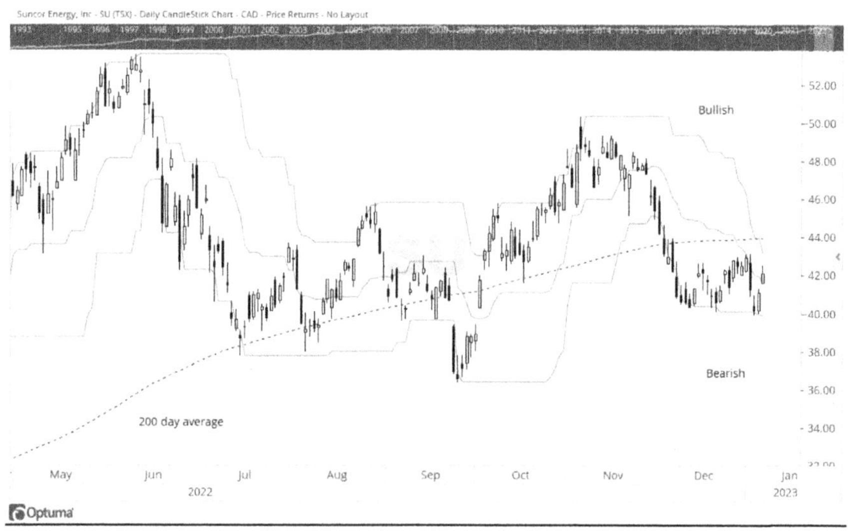

Figure 7-14

Suncor (SU) daily chart with Donchian Channels

The chart illustrates that in November there were two events where price moved above a prior swing peak. In both cases, a trader studying the RSI would not have been able to glean any confirmation of these bullish price moves. After the second of these moves, price pressed higher by nearly $3 per share. With price around the $27.50 level, the RSI was at or near the 70 level. Looking at subsequent price action, it becomes clear in hindsight that the RSI at 70 was signaling a stock that was perhaps overvalued and prone to having its price weaken.

The RSI offers little help to the trader seeking an indicator that will confirm bullish trend or bearish trend moves in conjunction with price surpassing prior peak and valley points. Perhaps the RSI held some deep meaning for Mr. Wilder in his day. But in this day and age of fast moving markets, there are better chart indicators to use than RSI.

Commodity Channel Index

The Commodity Channel Index was developed by trader Donald Lambert in the early 1980s. It compares the current price to the simple average of prices over a recent span of time. The CCI function is plotted on a vertical axis with a scale that ranges from -250 to +250.

The formula is:
$$CCI = \frac{(Price - simple\ average\ over\ past\ n\ periods)}{(0.015\ x\ mean\ deviation).}$$

The mean deviation (not to be confused with standard deviation) is calculated as the sum total of the absolute value of the differences between the current price divided by n.

Indicator readings that are deeply negative are suggestive that the prices have deviated sharply from average and that a trend change might be about to manifest. Readings strongly positive are suggestive of prices that have sharply deviated from their average and are poised to come down.

Figure 7-13 illustrates daily price action of Amazon (AMZN) with a 30-period Commodity Channel Index applied. Amazon, at this time of writing, remains mired in a bearish major trend.

By June 2022, price of Amazon shares had retraced a Fibonacci 78.6% of the overall advance from March 2020 to late November 2021. In July 2022, price action exhibited two moves above prior swing peaks. In each case the Commodity Channel Index value moved above the upper bound (100 level). The second of the two moves saw price gap higher and then continue to advance more. The CCI eventually reached the 200 mark and then began to fade. When the CCI crossed beneath the 100 upper bound, this signaled a peak in share price. This price rally was unable to surpass the 200-day average. The rally represented a Fibonacci 61.8% retracement of the April-May decline.

Following this failure to surpass the 200-day average, share price of Amazon drifted steadily lower into late December, halting at a 100% retracement of the March 2020 to late November 2021 advance.

In early January 2023, the CCI crossed above the lower bound (-100 line) to signal a trend change. In early February 2023, price had retraced a Fibonacci 48.6% of the August-December decline. Price again touched the 200-day average and lost momentum.

A trader using the Commodity Channel Index as a tool to indicate turning points in price should focus on moves of the CCI above the upper (+100) and lower (-100) bounds. Prior swing points should be observed and Fibonacci mathematics should be also used.

Donchian Channel

This indicator was developed in the 1960s by commodity trader Richard Donchian. The indicator comprises three lines: an upper bound, a lower bound, and an average of the two bound values. The upper bound is generally taken as the highest price in the past 20 periods. The lower bound is the lowest price in the past 20 periods.

What Mr. Donchian likely derived from the indicator was when price action touched the upper bound line, he would be alert for price to continue trending and hugging the bound line. When price action pulled away from the upper bound line, he would use a cross of the average line to decide whether to stay in the trade or not.

Figure 7-14 illustrates the daily price action of Canadian oilsands producer Suncor (TSX/NYSE: SU) with Donchian channel (n=20).

Perhaps Mr. Donchian enjoyed success with this indicator in the 1960s markets. In today's fast moving markets, the Donchian Channel offers little to the trader seeking to capitalize on trend changes.

Derivative Oscillator & Ergodic Oscillator

The Ergodic Oscillator makes use of the Ergodic Indicator. The Ergodic Indicator is the True Strength Index (discussed earlier in this chapter) developed by trader William Blau. The mathematics of the Ergodic Oscillator apply a 25-period exponential moving average (EMA) smoothing to the True Strength Index. The smoothed data is then smoothed again by calculating a 13-period EMA. Lastly a 7-period EMA of the smoothed data is calculated to act as a signal line. The difference between the 13-period smoothed data and the signal line is plotted as histogram bars. When the histogram crosses above the zero line on the plot, a buy signal is created. Histogram bars crossing below the zero line point to a sell signal. Traders will often adjust the settings to suit the volatility of a particular stock or futures contract. I prefer to use the standard settings of 25/13/7. This oscillator is regarded by many as being among the top ten chart indicators for identifying trend changes.

Not every software program will include the Ergodic Oscillator. The

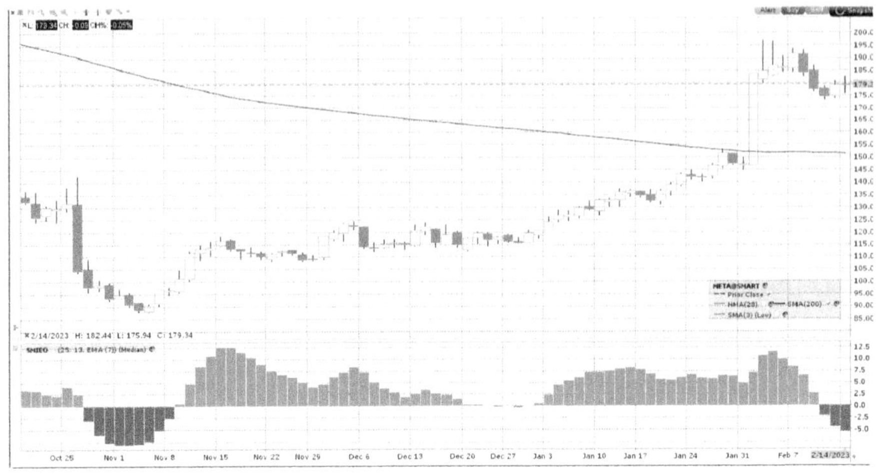

Figure 7-15

Meta (META) daily chart with Ergodic Oscillator

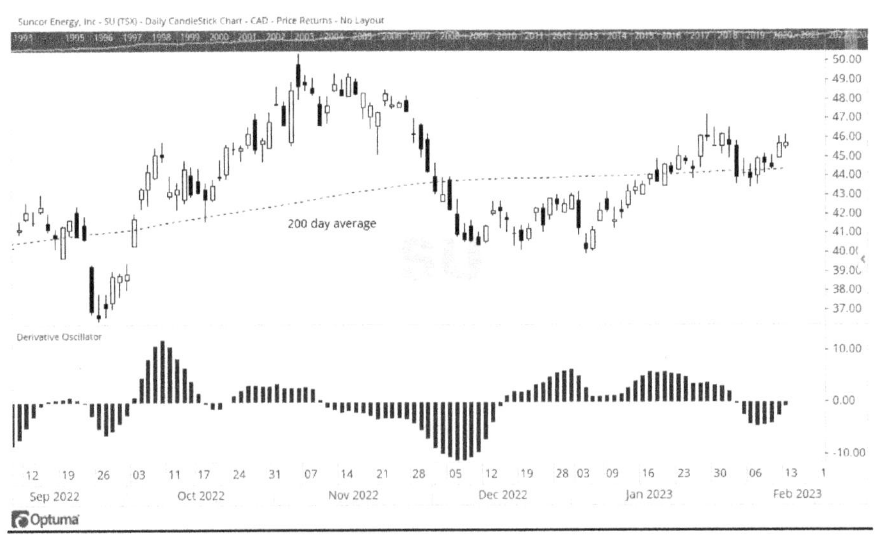

Figure 7-16

Suncor Energy (TSX:SU) daily chart with Derivative Oscillator

OPTUMA platform being used to generate charts for this manuscript does not contain the Ergodic Oscillator. However, my Interactive Brokers platform does have the Ergodic Oscillator. Figure 7-15 illustrates a chart of Meta (formerly Facebook). By November 2022, analysts were claiming to be thoroughly confused on the decision by META to embrace the metaverse. Share price had declined to the touch $88 on November 4. But, suddenly price started to rebound. This low reversal point came at a Fibonacci 78.6% retracement of the overall move from the 2012 IPO to the September peak at $382.

Figure 7-15 illustrates daily price action on META. Shortly after recording the 78.6% retracement, price action began to improve and the Ergodic Oscillator histogram bars move above the zero line indicating that the trend had changed. In early February 2023, META price momentum faded as price completed a Fibonacci 38.2% retracement of the decline from September 2021. The Ergodic Oscillator histogram bars slipped to beneath the zero line, confirming that the trend had changed.

If your software platform does not have the Ergodic Oscillator as a standard feature, it might have the Derivative Oscillator.

This trend change indicator was developed by Australian trader and author Constance Brown.

The starting point for this function is an RSI calculation:
$$RSI = 100 - 100/(1+RS) \text{ ; where}$$

$$RS = \frac{\text{(average gains over the past n periods)}}{\text{(average losses over the past n periods)}}$$

The data is then double smoothed by applying two exponential moving averages. A signal line is also created. The difference between the smoothed data and the signal line is plotted as histogram bars.

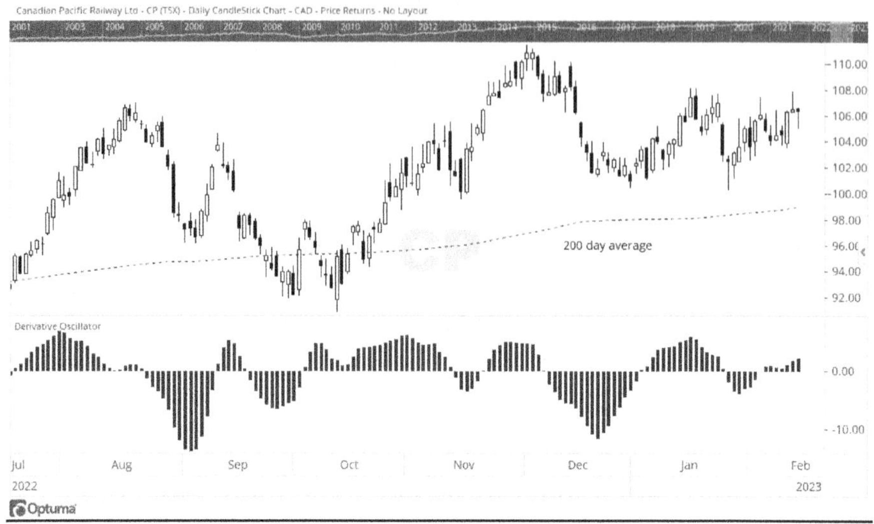

Figure 7-17

CP Rail (TSX:CP) daily chart with Derivative Oscillator

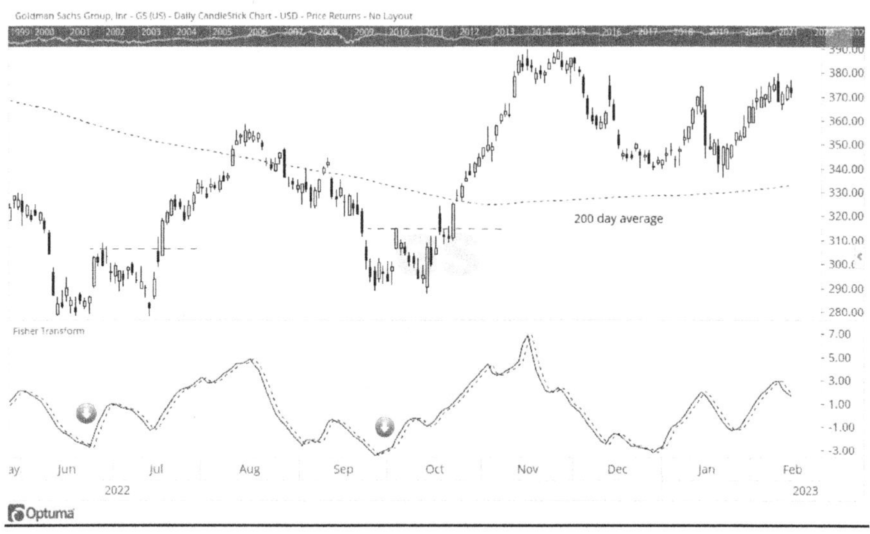

Figure 7-18

Goldman Sachs (GS) daily chart with the Fisher transform

Figure 7-16 presents daily price data for Canadian energy giant Suncor (TSX/NYSE:SU). The period covered by this chart segment is from June 2022 through February 2023. Price of Suncor shares trended higher from August 2021 through early June 2022. By late September 2022, price had retraced Fibonacci 48.6% of this move. With this retracement complete at the $36.50 area, price started to reverse and point higher. The Derivative Oscillator captured this change of trend, but the histogram bars did not get above the zero line until the $41 mark. A trader strictly following this indicator would have left $4 of potential profit on the table.

The price rally ran out of momentum in early October once price had retraced 100% of the September decline. However, the histogram bars were still well above the zero line and were not offering any suggestion of a coming price pullback. Price pulled back to touch the 200-day average taking the histogram bars beneath the zero line for two days. Price then began to recover and the bars resumed their standing above the zero line. As price rallied further, the height of the bars remained low. This likely cast a cautionary note on any trade that had been taken. In early November, price momentum faded as price completed a Fibonacci 78.6% retracement of the June through September decline. The oscillator bars moving below the zero line confirmed the change of trend, but this confirmation came several days after the actual price peak.

As of mid-February, the price of SU shares was struggling to surpass the Fibonacci 61.8% retracement of the November-December decline. The histogram bars were poised to get above the zero line. The histogram bars did eventually get above the zero line, just in time for SU shares to record a 78.6% retracement of the November-December decline. A trader acting on the histogram bars alone would have been met with a swift $9 per share drawdown.

The chart in Figure 7-17 illustrates price action on Canadian railway operator CP Rail (TSX:CP). The chart has been fitted with the Derivative Oscillator.

In July 2022, price started to move higher. A trader seeking to take a long position could have done so as the oscillator bars took on positive values above the zero line. As price reached a peak (and a 100% retracement of the recent decline) the histogram bars were still above the zero line although they were small in height. By the time the bars dipped below the zero line, price had already declined by over $2 per share. Price then declined to the $98 level. By the time the bars were again above the zero line, price was already at another interim peak. A trader relying strictly on the oscillator bars would have gotten badly whipsawed.

At the right side of Figure 7-17, in late December, price had declined a Fibonacci 48.6% retracement of the October through late November advance. The oscillator bars moving above the zero line confirmed that the trend was changing. However, a trader strictly watching the bars would have been late exiting a trade in January. By the time the bars fell beneath the zero line, price had fully retreated to erase any trade gains.

My stance is that the Ergodic Oscillator is far superior to the Derivative Oscillator. If your software platform does not provide you with the Ergodic Oscillator, consider just using the True Strength Index.

Fisher Transform

The use of *Fisher transform* mathematics in the context of the stock market is credited to trader John Ehlers. The Fisher transform mathematical technique was developed around 1921 by British mathematician and statistician Sir Ronald Aylmer Fisher. His mathematical approach was used to transform (x, y) data points into a Gaussian (normal-bell curved) distribution. Ehlers realized that (x, y) data points could be taken as (price, time) data points from a stock or commodity chart.

> Fisher's method developed in 1921 starts with calculating the correlation coefficient (r) between x and y using the formula:

$$r = \text{cov}\,(x, y) \,/\, (\sigma\,x)(\sigma\,y)\,;$$

where cov refers to the statistical covariance
and σ refers to standard deviation.

The actual transformation formula created a normally distributed variable (z) using the formula:

$$z = \ln\,(1+r)/(1-r).$$

In John Ehlers approach, there are five calculation steps involved: a mid-point calculation, an intermediate calculation, a smoothing, a Fisher transform, and a final smoothing.

1) Determination of mid-point is calculated as
the average between the high and the low price
as seen over the n-period timeframe.

2) Intermediate data is arrived at by the following formula·

3) Intermediate = 2 x [(mid-point-lowest
data point)/(highest – lowest)]

4) The Intermediate data is smoothed by
applying a 5-period EMA.

5) A Fisher transform is applied to the Intermediate data using
the following:
Fisher = logarithm [(1+smoothed data)/(1-smoothed data)]

6) A 3-period EMA is applied to the Fisher
data to create a signal line.

Ehlers approach to interpreting the plotted output is to focus on the extremes of the plot. When the output plot is at or near a maximum, there is a very good chance that the trend is about to change from bullish

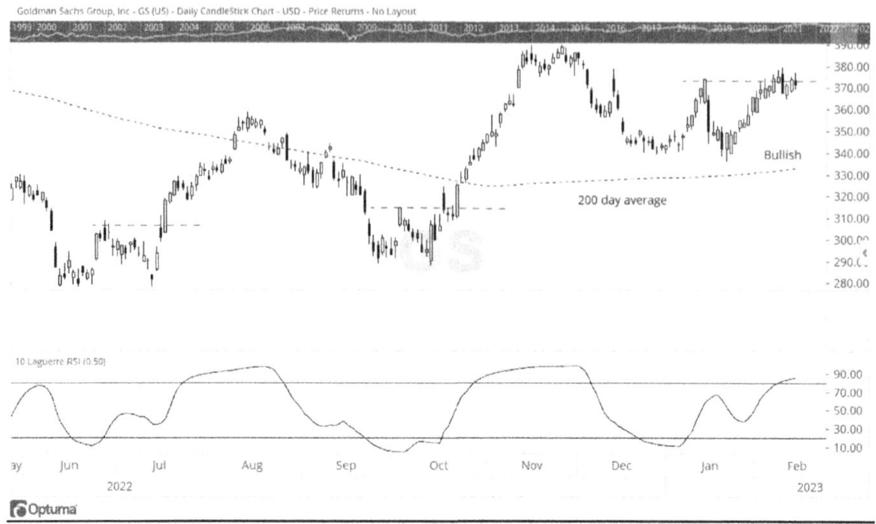

Figure 7-19

Goldman Sachs (GS) daily chart with the Laguerre transform

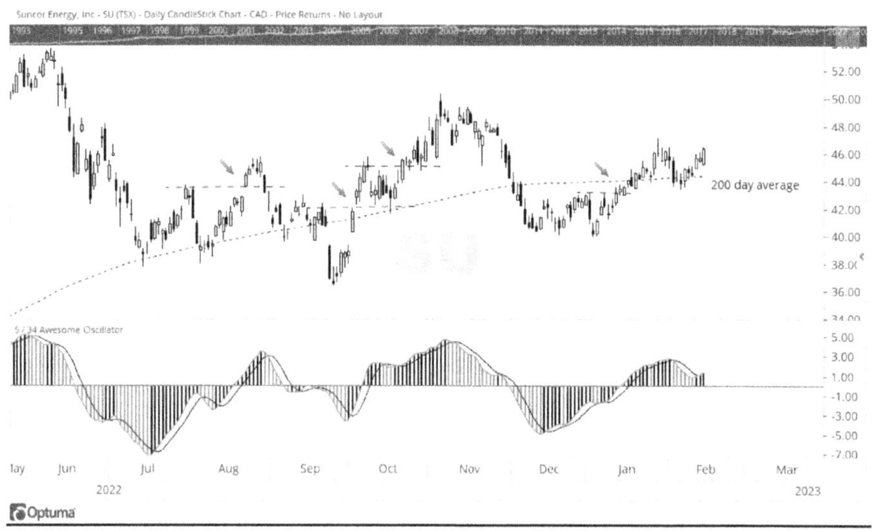

Figure 7-20

Suncor (TSX:SU) daily chart with the Awesome Oscillator

to bearish. When the output plot is at or near a minimum, there is a very good chance that the trend is about to change from bearish to bullish.

Figure 7-18 illustrates daily price action of Goldman Sachs shares (GS) from June 2022 through mid-February 2023. The lower pane of the chart has been fitted with the Fisher transform indicator. The solid line is the transform function, the dashed line is the signal line. A bullish signal is created as the indicator line crosses the signal line.

The lower pane in Figure 7-18 has been overlaid with two arrow symbols that denote Fisher transform buy signals at price lows. A trader strictly following these signals would have found, in both cases, price rolling over and doubling back on itself. The horizontal dashed lines denote trade entry points that align to prior swing peaks. Initiating a trade at these points would have been far more prudent.

At the right side of the chart, in early January 2023, the Fisher transform again gave a positive crossover. However, price advanced and then rolled over on itself before advancing again.

The Fisher transform does a credible job of helping the trader identify potential trend changes. However, caution must be taken if relying exclusively on the indicator.

Laguerre RSI

The *Laguerre RSI* was also created by trader John Ehlers. He applied a mathematical technique called a Laguerre transform to RSI data points. The Laguerre transform method is credited to French mathematician Edmond Laguerre who rose to prominence in the mid-1800s. Laguerre's approach sought to smooth out scientific data into an easier-to-analyze wave function.

Figure 7-19 illustrates the same Goldman Sachs chart as in Figure 7-18,

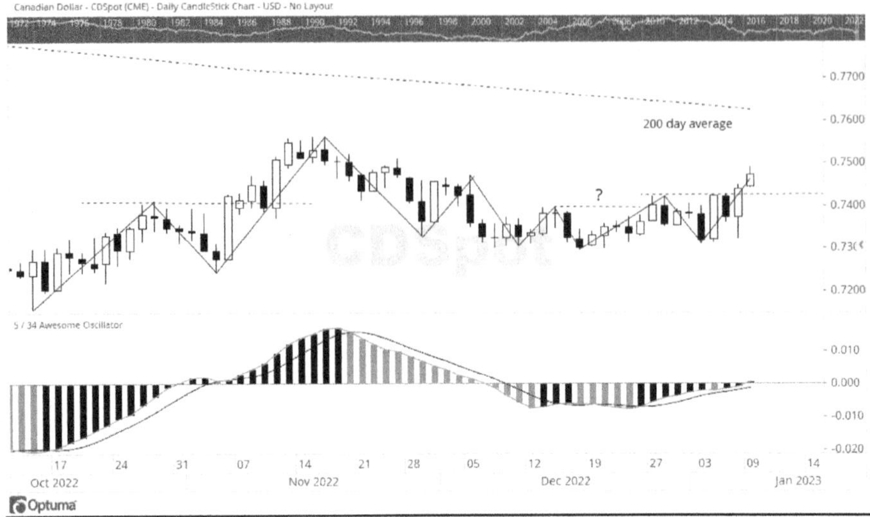

Figure 7-21

Canadian Dollar futures (continuous front month) daily chart with the Awesome Oscillator

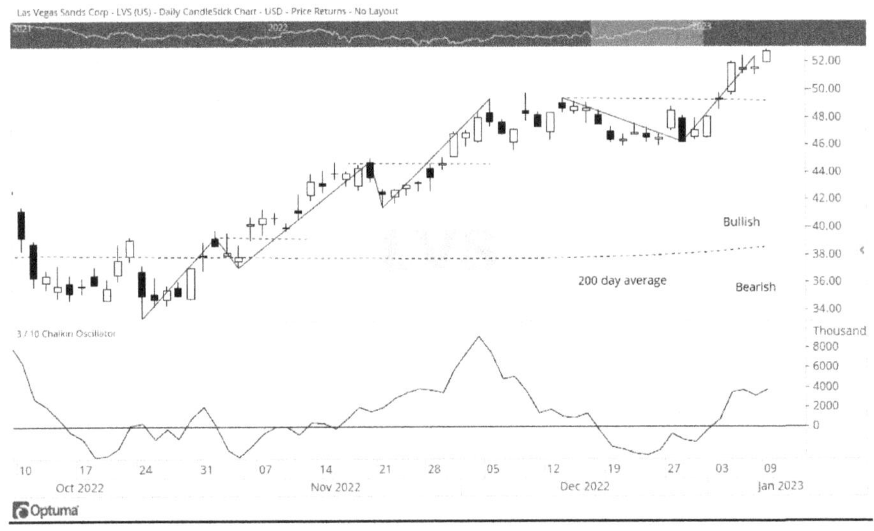

Figure 7-22

Las Vegas Sands (LSV) daily chart with Chaikin Oscillator

except with a Laguerre RSI function based on a 10-period lookback (n=10) applied. The Laguerre function is plotted on a vertical scale running from 0 to 100.

At each of the two prior peak events in July and October 2022, the 10-period Laguerre transform indicator validated the trade as it crossed above its upper bound. However, in both cases, the validation came later than the actual surpassing of the prior swing point.

The Laguerre transform does a credible job of helping the trader identify potential trend changes. However, caution must be taken if relying exclusively on the indicator.

Awesome Oscillator

The Awesome Oscillator was developed by trader Bill Williams. Mathematically, it is the difference between a 5-bar moving average and a 34-bar simple moving average (SMA). The value for each bar or candlestick is taken as the *median* (mid-point) between the high and the low price points of the bar.

The formula is:
Oscillator = 5-period SMA minus 34-period SMA.

A trader using the prior swing peak methodology would watch this oscillator for zero line crossovers. The oscillator crossing above the zero line should act as conformation that price is about to surpass a prior swing value.

Figure 7-20 illustrates daily price action on Canadian energy giant Suncor. The chart has been fitted with the Awesome Oscillator. Figure 7-20 also contains four incidents where price surpassed a prior peak. In three of the four cases, the Awesome Oscillator crossed over the zero line a couple days later than the actual event of price surpassing a prior swing high.

A trader strictly following this oscillator could have used it to initiate trades as it crossed above the zero line. However, a trader seeking earlier trade entry signals would want to use a different indicator.

Figure 7-21 illustrates daily price action on the Canadian dollar. The chart has been fitted with the Awesome Oscillator. In early November 2022, the oscillator moved above the zero line, tentatively signaling a buying opportunity. A trader taking a long futures position on this indication would soon have realized that the oscillator had prompted a buy signal too early. The Canadian dollar subsequently fell from 0.7340 to 0.7240 for a drawdown of $1000 on the trade.

However, price subsequently rebounded and surpassed a swing peak that had been created on October 24. The bars of the oscillator were still above the zero line at this point.

The key observation is that the Awesome Oscillator might not be so awesome after all with its propensity for poor trade entry timing signals.

Chaikin Oscillator

The Chaikin Oscillator was developed by trader Marc Chaikin. It uses a comparison of two moving averages: a 3-day average and a 10-day average. But the averages are not calculated from price alone. Rather, the averages are of a construct called the Accumulation Distribution Line (A/D Line). The A/D Line is in itself a trend indicator. For example, if the price of a stock is falling in value, but the A/D Line starts turning and heading higher, this is a hint that the price trend of the stock might be about to change. The A/D Line is further unique in that it considers share trading volume as part of its calculation.

The A/D Line calculation depends on two individual formulas for its determination:

$$(1)\ \text{Money Flow Multiplier (MFM)} = \frac{[(\text{Close} - \text{Low})\ \text{minus}\ (\text{High-Close})]}{(\text{High-Low})}$$

(2) Money Flow Volume (MFV) =
MFM x share volume for the period being studied.

The A/D Line is then calculated as:
A/D Line = previous period A/D + current period MFV.

The Chaikin methodology subtracts the 10-day EMA of the A/D Line from the 3-day EMA of the A/D line. The result of this difference is then plotted.

The Chaikin Oscillator experienced a revival in 2022 when the owner of a US-based newsletter publishing company began marketing Mr. Chaikin and his oscillator through various on-line newsletter publications. In an effort to attract new subscribers, they made his indicator sound like a fool-proof way of making money on the stock market. Mr. Chaikin was presented as a wealthy Wall Street player who now just wanted to do the right thing for the average investor. The implied message was if his indicator had made him wealthy, it could do likewise for you. Needless to say, I greeted this marketing effort with a healthy dose of skepticism.

Figure 7-22 illustrates price action on casino operator Las Vegas Sands (LSV) from October 2022 to January 2023. The lower pane of the chart has been fitted with the Chaikin Oscillator. The chart has been overlaid with three occurrences of price surpassing a prior peak. There is no alignment between these swing peak trade signals and the oscillator. In fact, there is obvious inconsistency. Mathematically, this inconsistency arises due to the volume term in the Money Flow Volume (MFV) equation. For traders whose software platforms come equipped with the Chaikin Oscillator,

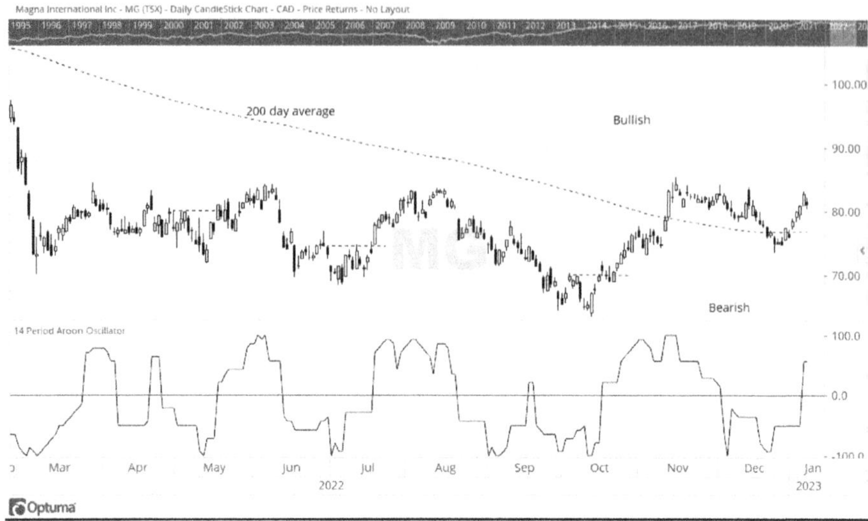

Figure 7-23

Magna (TSX:MG) with Aroon Oscillator

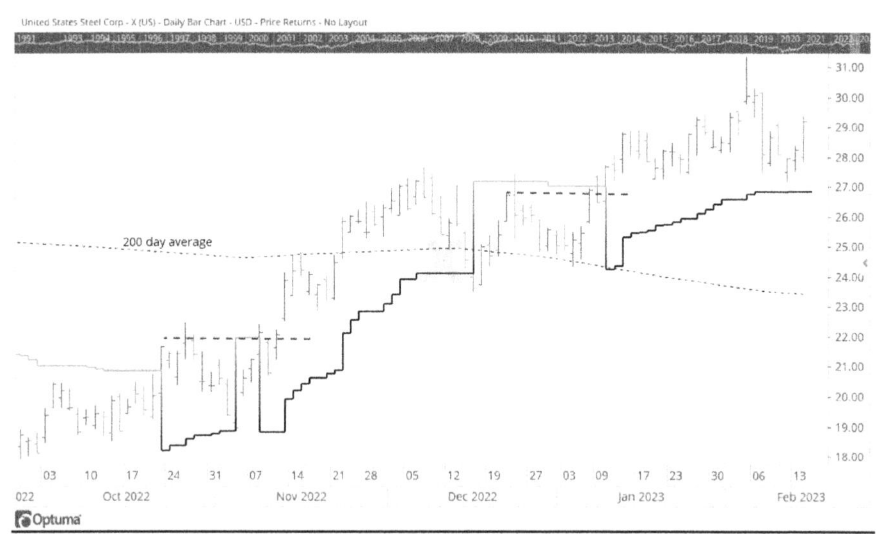

Figure 7-24

US Steel (X) with Wilder Volatility Stop

caution is advised. There are other indicators that are more effective at assisting with trading.

Aroon Oscillator

The Aroon oscillator was developed in the 1990s by trader Tushar Chande. The name *Aroon* is a taken from the Sanskrit language and means *dawn's early light.*

The formula is:
Aroon oscillator = Aroon up – Aroon down;
where Aroon up = 100* [(n - periods since the n period high)/n];
where Aroon down = 100* [(n - periods since the n period low)/n].

The period *n* is usually a default of 25 bars or candlesticks in most software market programs. The chart in Figure 7-23 illustrates price action on Canadian-headquartered automotive parts manufacturer Magna (TSX:MG). The chart has been fitted with the Aroon Oscillator using a *n* value of 14 periods, instead of the default of 25 periods.

Figure 7-23 has been overlaid with three occasions of price surpassing a prior peak. A trader strictly following the Aroon Oscillator would buy shares in Magna when the oscillator value was crossing up and through the zero line. The risk with this approach is that any subsequent rise in price could fall back on itself, sending the trader scrambling to exit the trade. The other risk is that any subsequent rise in price proves to be insignificantly small. However, as Figure 7-23 shows, on balance the Aroon Oscillator appears to work reasonably well as an indicator of a pending trend change.

In May 2022, the oscillator probed the minus 100 level; a suggestion that trend would change. Indeed, it did; price moved from a low of $72 to a peak of $84 in June. Along the way, price surpassed a prior swing peak. As this occurred, the Aroon Oscillator passed through the zero level.

A similar situation developed in July. The oscillator was near the minus 100 level and price then started to trend higher. A trader could have taken a long position at this point. Along the way, price surpassed a prior swing peak. As this occurred, the Aroon Oscillator passed through the zero level.

In September, a similar situation again occurred. However, this time a trader taking a long position with the Aroon Oscillator at a low level would have been met with only a tepid price advance. There was no prior swing peak to focus on.

In October, the oscillator was again at a low level, hinting that a trend change was at hand. Price had just completed a Fibonacci 61.8% retracement of the move from March 2020 to the price peak in June 2021. A trader with a more cautious mindset might have decided to wait for price to surpass the October 6 swing peak. As price moved above this swing level, the oscillator crossed the zero line to validate the trade.

At the right side of the chart, price can be seen moving higher and the oscillator has moved through the zero level. On a closing price basis, price has surpassed the prior swing peak point.

The Aroon Oscillator appears to be a good trend indicator tool to use. Ideally one will want to use it in conjunction with the prior swing methodology and Fibonacci mathematics.

Wilder Volatility Stop

When my Branch Manager was reminding me to "follow the trend" back in my broker/investment advisor days, it was because of his results using software that parsed price data through a trend model based on Welles Wilder's mathematics.

In the late 1970s, Wilder published a book entitled *New Concepts in Technical Trading* in which he described his *Volatility Stop* indicator. The

Volatility Stop uses a mathematical construct called *Average True Range* (ATR). The True Range is defined as being the *greatest* of one of the following:

- current high less the current low;

- the absolute value of the current high less the previous close;

- the absolute value of the current low less the previous close.

The ATR is a moving average of a series of True Ranges. Wilder used n=7 price bars to calculate the ATR for use in his Volatility Stop.

Wilder next multiplied the ATR by a constant number. His testing showed that the best range for this constant was between 2.8 and 3.1. The result of ATR x constant is what Wilder called ARC value.

Wilder then suggested that a long trade be exited if and when price fell beneath the most significant closing price for the recent 7 bars minus ARC. A short trade should be exited if and when price gets above the most significant closing price for the recent 7 bars plus ARC. On a typical stock chart with the Wilder Volatility Stop overlaid, one will see a blue line and a red line. The blue line indicates that the trend is bullish. As the blue line transitions to red, the trend is turning bearish. In this black and white manuscript, the darker black parts of the Volatility Stop are what would appear in blue (bullish) on a computer monitor. The lighter gray parts of the Volatility Stop are what would appear in red (bearish) on a computer monitor.

Figure 7-24 illustrates daily price action on US Steel (NYSE:X). The Wilder Volatility Stop has been overlaid using n=7 bars and the constant multiplier = 3.0.

In late October 2022, the Volatility Stop offered indication that the trend on US Steel had changed from bearish to bullish. However, the Gartley

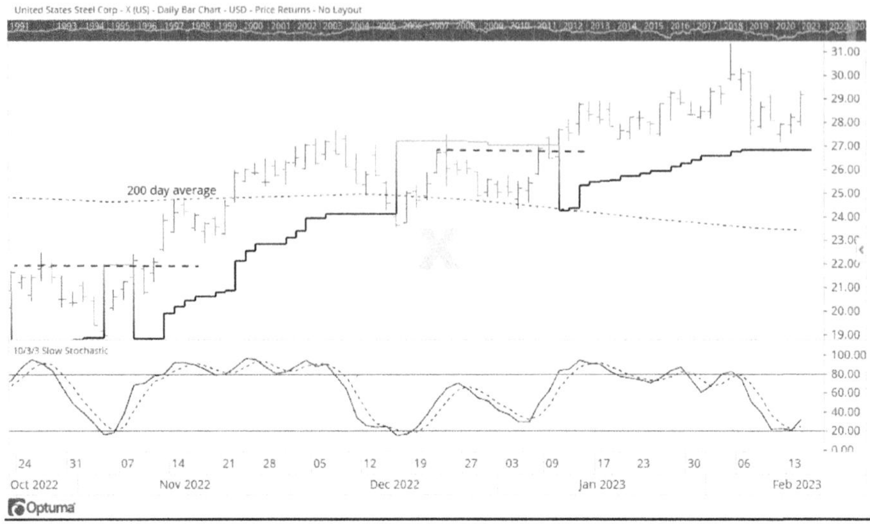

Figure 7-25

US Steel (X) with Wilder Volatility Stop and Slow Stochastic

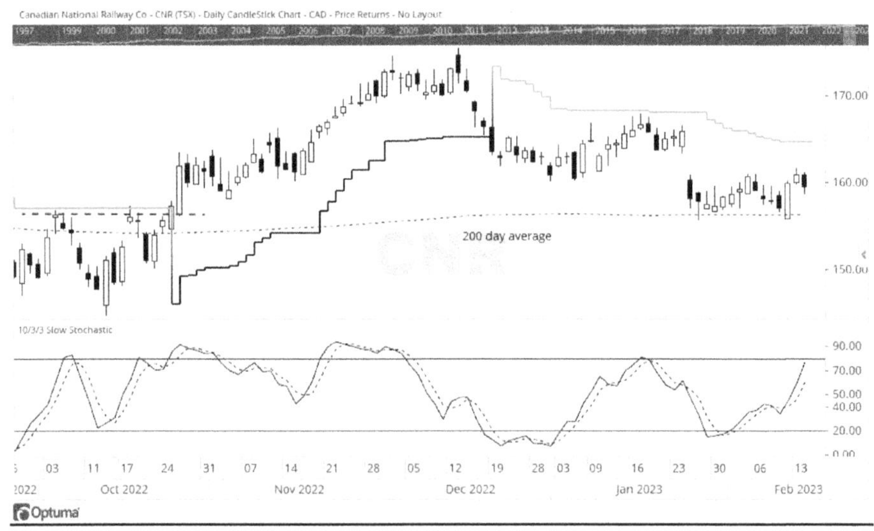

Figure 7-26

CN Rail (TSX: CNR) with Wilder Volatility Stop

major trend on US Steel (as defined by price relative to the 200-day average) was still bearish. The implication here is that the Volatility Stop will identify trend changes well in advance of the Gartley method. It is also interesting to note that as the Volatility Stop offered the trend change indication, share price was surpassing a swing peak from October 5.

On December 15, the Volatility Stop changed color, signaling that the price trend on US Steel had turned bearish. Herein is an aspect of the Volatility Stop that demands attention. Note that price had completely reversed itself by the time the Volatility Stop had changed color. Traders and investors using the Wilder Volatility Stop must focus on the 'constant' value. It cannot be input as 2.9, for example. Each stock being analyzed with the Wilder Stop will demand a unique 'constant' value. Over time, as news flow and circumstances contribute to greater or lesser share price volatility, the 'constant' value may require minor adjusting.

On January 10, 2023 the Volatility Stop indicator again exhibited a change of color. Notice that at the same time, price was surpassing a prior swing peak. Price went on to rally from the $27 level to a high of $31. At this time of writing, the Volatility Stop is showing the trend to still be bullish, even though price has retreated from the $31 high.

Figure 7-25 is the same as Figure 7-24, except that the Slow Stochastic has been added in the lower pane window in the chart. Looking at the far-left side of the chart, the Slow Stochastic surpassed its upper bound one day after the Volatility Stop pointed to a trend change. On December 7, as price was testing the $27 level, the Stochastic rolled over and moved beneath the upper bound. This was a signal that something was wrong; the trend was about to change. Yet, the Volatility Stop offered no suggestion of a trend change.

From mid-December through early January 2023, the Volatility Stop did not offer any trend change signals. The Stochastic, meantime, bounced along between its upper and lower bounds and offered no trade indications either. On January 10, a day after price had surpassed a prior swing peak, the Volatility Stop pointed to a trend change. So too did the Stochastic as it moved above its upper bound. On February 7, price dipped sharply, sending the Stochastic beneath its upper bound. However, the Volatility Stop was continuing to show a positive trend. The implication here is that traders and investors give thought to their objectives. If the objective is short-term trading, using the Volatility Stop in conjunction with the Slow Stochastic is a prudent approach. If the time horizon is a bit longer, and if some price volatility can be withstood, the use of the Volatility Stop by itself is a good approach, providing due attention is paid to the 'constant' value.

Figure 7-26 presents another example of a chart fitted with the Wilder Volatility Stop and the Slow Stochastic. The stock illustrated in Figure 7-26 is Canadian railway operator CN Rail (TSX/NYSE:CNR).

In late October 2022, the Wilder Volatility Stop signaled the arrival of a bullish trend. At the same time, the Slow Stochastic moved above its upper bound. Price moved above a prior swing high from the week prior.

On November 1, the Stochastic moved beneath its upper bound. Share price drifted sideways until mid-November when the Stochastic again moved above its upper bound signaling a resumption of the bullish trend. Meanwhile, the Volatility Stop had not wavered. A trader exclusively following it would have been kept in a long trade position.

On December 2, after price had tested the $175 level, the Stochastic moved beneath its upper bound, signaling it was time to exit any long positions. However, the Volatility Stop continued to suggest a bullish trend was in place right up until December 19. By that time, $12 of profit had disappeared for a trader strictly following the Volatility Stop.

Having studied numerous stock and commodity charts in the context of the Wilder Volatility Stop, my conclusion is that it is a powerful indicator. However, in today's fast-moving markets, if the investment objective is short-term trading, the Volatility Stop ideally should be used in conjunction with another indicator such as a Stochastic. If some price volatility can be tolerated and if the investment horizon is a bit longer, the Volatility Stop can be used along. However, the 'constant' value might require periodic adjusting.

CHAPTER 8
SHORT-TERM CHARTS AND THE TREND

The previous chapters examined a wider variety of different technical indicators. Some were shown to be very effective at helping to identify changes in trend; some were shown to be less effective. All were presented in the context of daily charts.

This chapter aims to illustrate the application of some of these indicators to hourly charts for the benefit of traders with a shorter time horizon.

Percent Price Oscillator

Figure 8-1 illustrates hourly price action on United Airlines (UAL) between December 7, 2022 and January 30, 2023. The chart has been fitted with a 55-bar moving average (recall that 55 is a Fibonacci number). The chart has also been fitted with the Precent Price Oscillator (PPO).

From December 7 to January 3, the short term trend was bearish with price action recording a series of lower tops. On January 4, price moved above the 55-bar average and the PPO recorded a bullish crossover. The

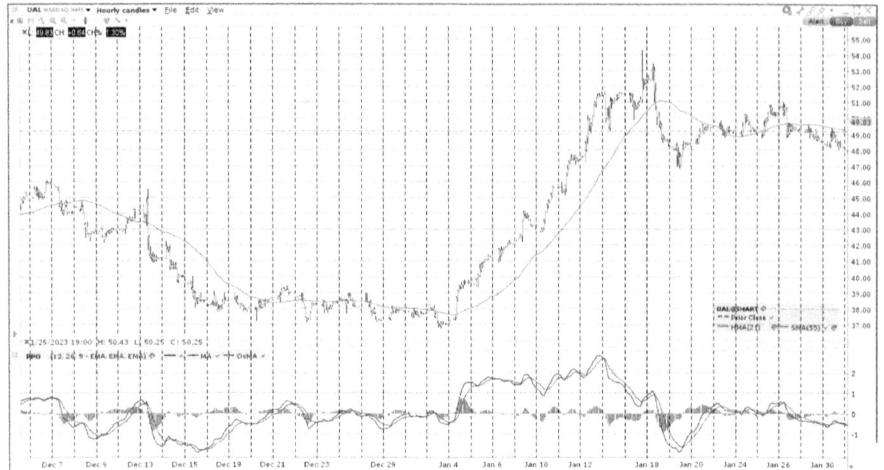

Figure 8-1

United Airlines (UAL) hourly chart with Percent Price Oscillator

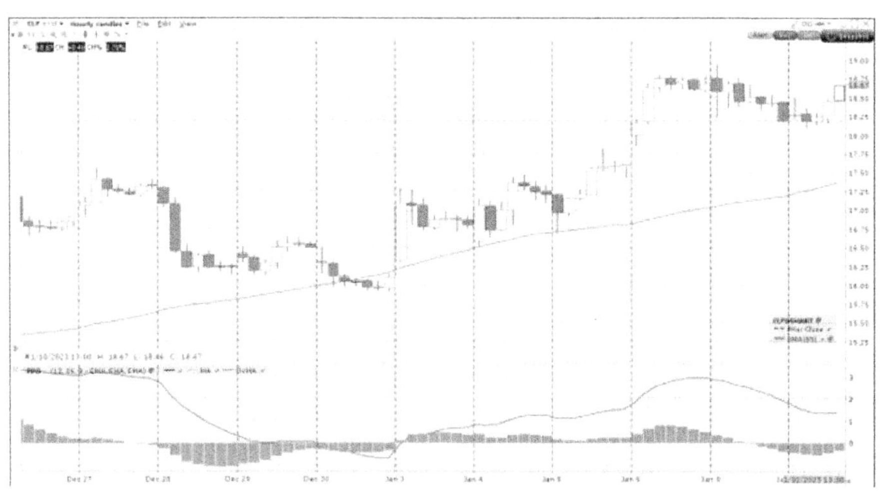

Figure 8-2

US Dollar futures (front month) hourly chart with Percent Price Oscillator

short term trend on the hourly chart had changed to bullish. On the heels of this hourly chart trend change, share price moved up to the $51 level. On the daily chart, price moved above the 200-day average to signal a bullish major trend.

Figure 8-2 illustrates hourly price action on the US Dollar futures for the first half of February 2023. On February 2, price moved above the 55-bar average. The Percent Price Oscillator (PPO) had recorded a positive crossover a day before. On February 7, price fell beneath the 55-bar average as the PPO recorded a negative crossover. Another PPO crossover came on February 9 and on February 10, price got above the 55-bar average and stayed there until February 13.

Fast Stochastic

Figure 8-3 illustrates an hourly chart of electric vehicle maker Tesla (TSLA) with the Fast Stochastic indicator applied. The timeframe covered by this chart is from December 23, 2022 to January 10, 2023.

In early January, the Fast Stochastic crossed its upper bound (80 level) just as price was poised to cross above the 55-bar moving average. The confluence of these two events signaled a trend change. A trader taking a long position on 100 shares would have enjoyed a tidy gain in the trade in a matter of hours.

True Strength Index

Figure 8-4 illustrates hourly price action on shares of the Ford Motor Company. The chart has been fitted with a 55-bar average and also the True Strength Index.

On December 29, the True Strength Index exhibited a bullish crossover. A trader taking a long position at this crossover would have enjoyed a decent gain from the $11.00 entry point. More bullish confirmation came on

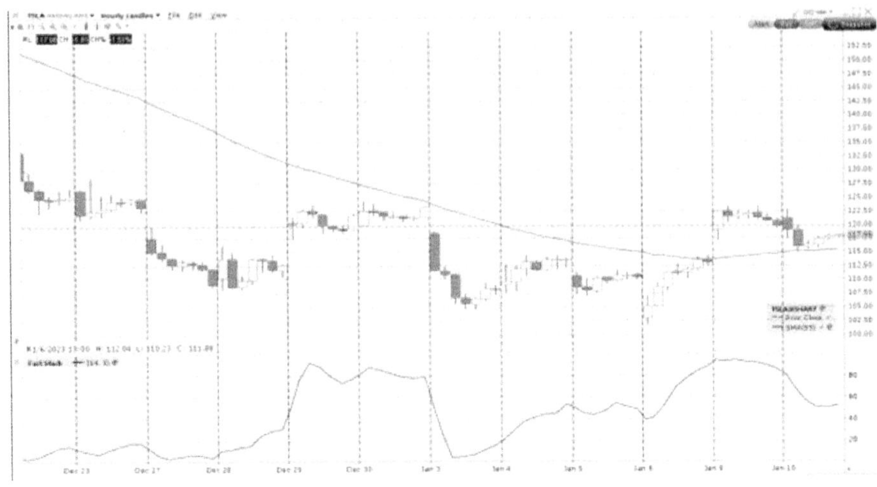

Figure 8-3

Tesla (TSLA) hourly chart with Fast Stochastic

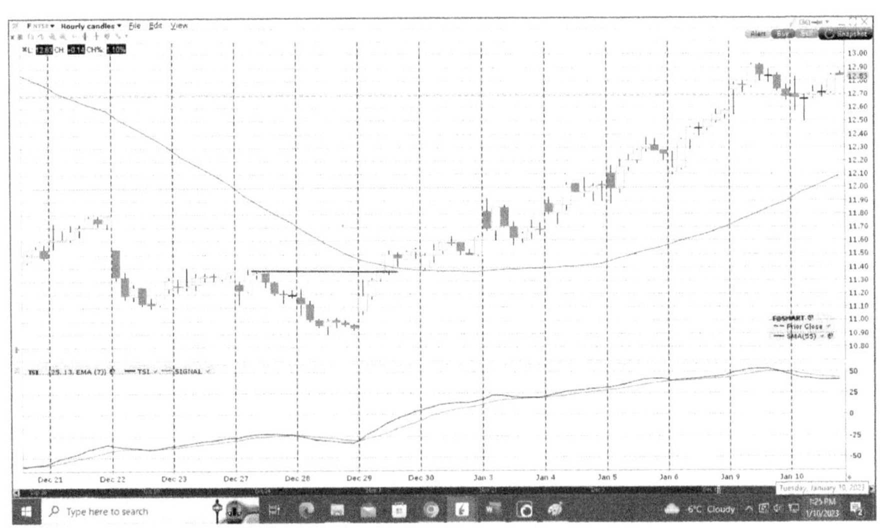

Figure 8-4

Ford Motors (F) hourly chart with True Strength Index

December 30 as price crossed above the 55-bar average. By the time the various indicators on the daily chart offered buy signals, a trader using the hourly chart would have been already well rewarded.

Ergodic Oscillator

Figure 8-5 illustrates hourly price action on shares of Brazilian-based, global mining company Vale (VALE). The chart has been fitted with a 55-bar average along with the Ergodic Oscillator developed by William Blau.

In December, price receded to test the 55-bar average. As price slowly started to ease higher, the oscillator histogram bars moved above the zero line to signal a trading opportunity. Over the next several trading sessions, price rose from the $14.40 level to the $17.10 level. At the $17.10 level, the histogram bars had diminished in height, suggesting a trend change was possibly at hand. Indeed, it was, and histogram bars soon turned below the zero line. In early January again, histogram bars moved above the zero line, signaling a trend change. A couple hourly bars later and price moved above the 55-bar average to confirm the trend change.

Awesome Oscillator

Figure 8-6 illustrates daily price action on Canadian heavy oil producer MEG Energy (TSX:MEG).

Figure 8-6 illustrates that on February 7, 2023 the oscillator pointed to a trade entry. Price also moved above the 55-bar average at the same time. A trader entering a long trade on February 7 would have realized a gain of nearly $1 per share by February 9.

Aroon Oscillator

In the daily chart discussion of the Aroon Oscillator, it was stated that it appears to be a good trend indicator tool to use either on a stand-alone

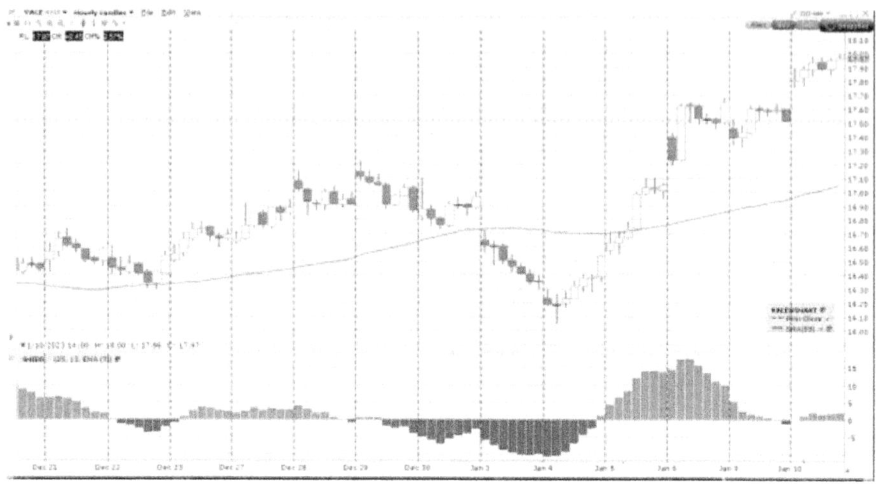

Figure 8-5

Vale (VALE) hourly chart with Ergodic Oscillator

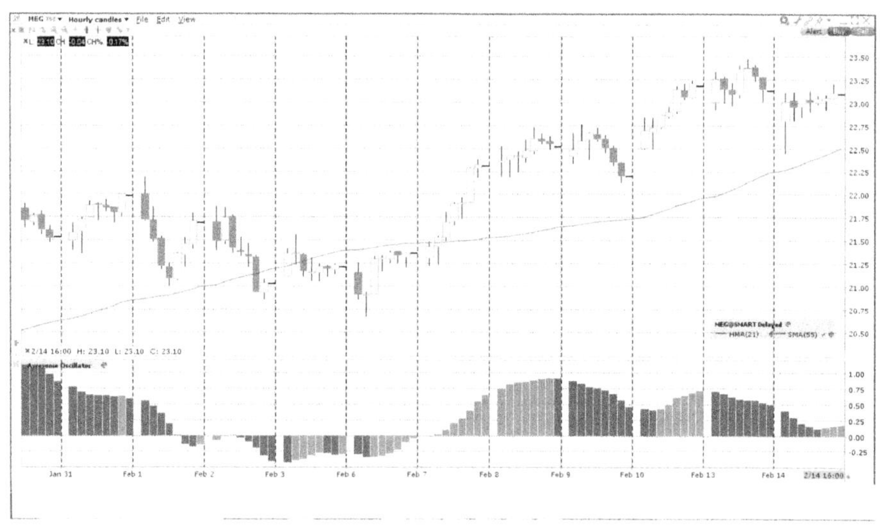

Figure 8-6

MEG Energy (MEG) hourly chart with Awesome Oscillator

basis or in conjunction with a swing trade strategy.

Continuing with the example of MEG Energy, Figure 8-7 shows the Aroon Oscillator applied to the hourly chart. This chart shows a number of points where the oscillator crosses up and through the zero line. Looking at these same times on a daily chart shows that a trader using a daily chart with something like a Slow Stochastic would have also identified these entry points. However, the Aroon Oscillator on an hourly chart provides much more precise entry points.

The Aroon Oscillator is a good trend change tool on an hourly chart basis.

Know Sure Thing (KST) Indicator

The Know Sure Thing (KST) indicator was developed by trader Martin Pring in the early 1990s. This indicator utilizes the concept of rate of change, as was discussed in the previous chapter. Figure 8-8 illustrates hourly price action on the E-mini Nasdaq futures March 2023 contract. The chart has been fitted with a 55-bar average as well as the KST indicator.

As Figure 8-8 shows, bullish crossovers on the KST indicator pointed to a trade entry point already on January 6, 2023. This was several days before indicators on a daily chart offered a buy signal.

The KST indicator is a valuable tool to use on an hourly chart configuration.

MAC-D

As discussed in a previous chapter, in 1979, technical chartist Gerald Appel considered the relationship between two exponential moving averages (EMA) of a series of price bars. The result was what he called the Moving Average Convergence Divergence (MAC-D) indicator.

As the E-mini Nasdaq hourly chart in Figure 8-9 shows, bullish crossovers

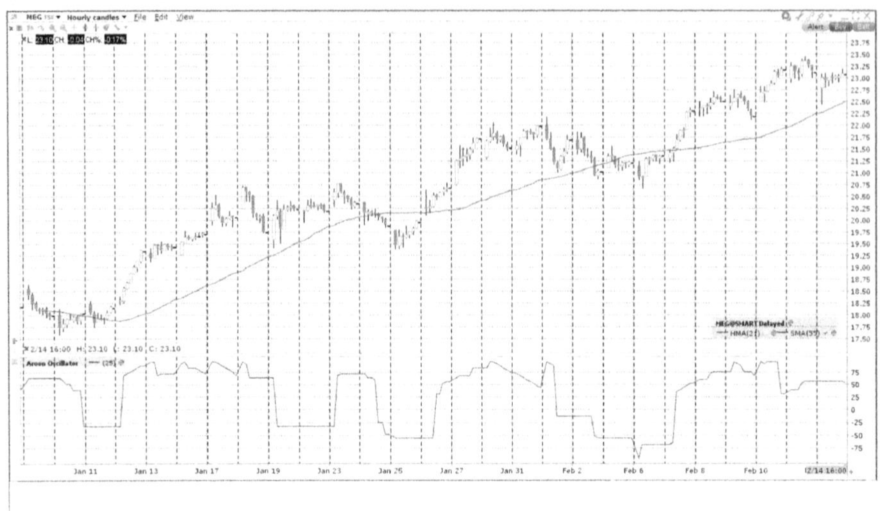

Figure 8-7

MEG Energy (MEG) hourly chart with Aroon Oscillator

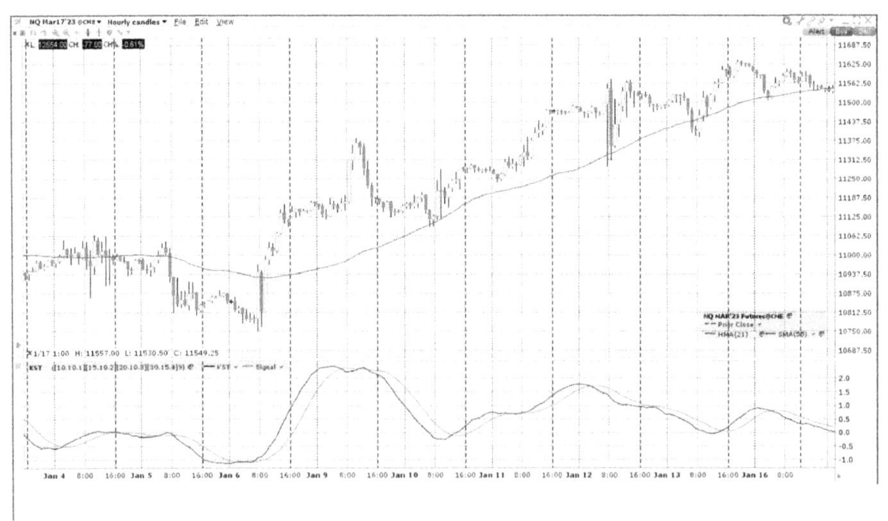

Figure 8-8

E-mini Nasdaq March 2023 contract hourly chart with KST Indicator

on the MAC-D indicator prove adept at identifying trade entry points on an hourly chart.

TRIX Indicator

As discussed in a previous chapter, TRIX is an acronym for the triple exponential average. The indicator is designed around a 15-period exponential moving average.

In a previous chapter, it was noted that on a daily chart setup the TRIX indicator proved itself a useful tool for identifying trend changes. Figure 8-10 illustrates the E-mini Nasdaq price action with the TRIX indicator in the lower pane on the chart. However, a problem immediately becomes apparent. The Interactive Brokers platform displays the TRIX indicator as a single line with no signal component. This oversight on the part of the software programmers is certainly disturbing. Regardless, Figure 8-10 does show that TRIX crossovers of the zero line do align to points where price moves markedly. A signal line would serve to make the TRIX indicator more functional.

To Sum Up

At the hourly chart level, my back-testing has shown that the KST, MAC-D, Percent Price Oscillator, Fast Stochastic, True Strength Index, Ergodic Oscillator, Awesome Oscillator, and Aroon Oscillator are all valuable resources to help discern short term trend changes.

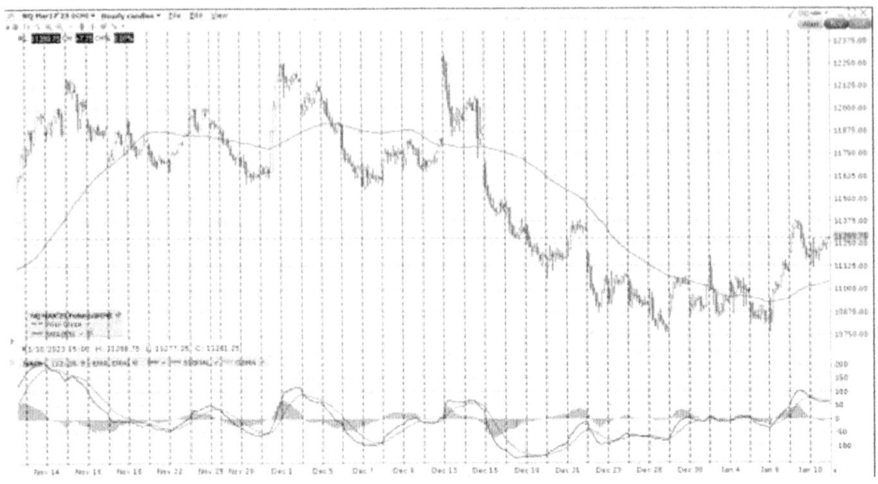

Figure 8-9

E-mini Nasdaq March 2023 contract hourly chart with MAC-D Indicator

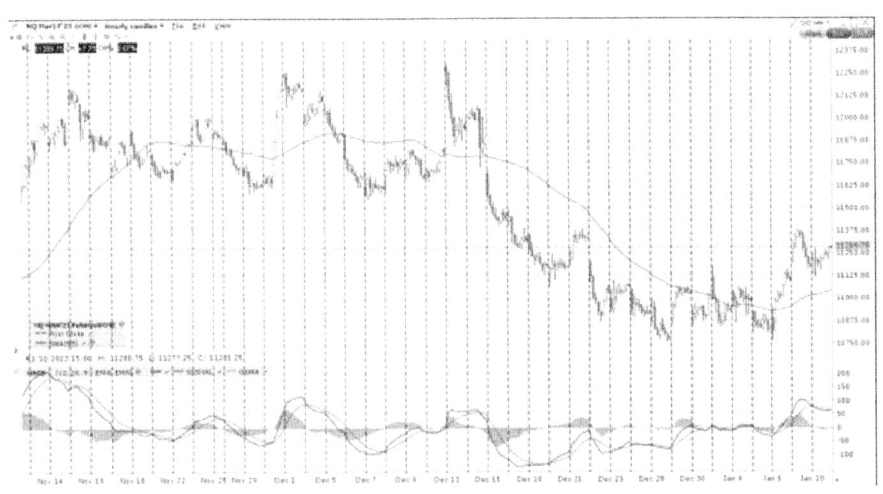

Figure 8-10

E-mini Nasdaq March 2023 contract hourly chart with TRIX Indicator

CHAPTER 9
LONGER-TERM CHARTS AND THE TREND

The previous chapters have focused on market participants with a shorter-term horizon. This chapter is focused on the investor; someone with a longer-term horizon. Someone who is *not* checking stock charts and indices every single day. This chapter presents some of the indicators that I have found that work well in the context of a weekly price chart.

KST Indicator

Figure 9-1 illustrates a weekly chart of Amazon (AMZN). The chart has been overlaid with a 40-week moving average. Up until November 2021, share price was trending higher, making higher lows as it went. In late December, price ($175 range) breached the 40-week average and the KST indicator slipped beneath the zero line.

To an investor with a longer horizon, the KST indicator and 40-week average negative crossovers in late 2021 signaled a problem. As of February 2023, Amazon shares have continued trending lower, punctuated along the way with periodic counter-trend rallies that have all failed to surpass

Figure 9-1

Amazon (AMZN) weekly chart with KST indicator

Figure 9-2

American Airlines (AAL) weekly chart with KST indicator

the 40-week average. As of February 2023, that same investor would still be looking for share price to surpass the 40-week average and for the KST indicator to offer confirmation of a trend change.

Figure 9-2 illustrates the weekly chart of American Airlines (AAL) with a 40-week average and the KST indicator. Airlines have been struggling with a variety of staffing and logistical issues for some time now. Figure 9-2 shows that an investor should have exited AAL shares in July 2021 as price fell beneath the 40-week average. This move was confirmed by the KST indicator falling beneath the zero line.

MAC-D

The COVID pandemic spurred some technology companies to dizzying price heights. Instead of physically meeting with a person to obtain document signatures, why not do it online? Figure 9-3 illustrates weekly price action of online document signing company DocuSign (DOCU). In March 2021, price breaking beneath the 40-week average and the MAC-D providing a negative crossover was an early warning that online document processing was perhaps falling out of favor. In September 2021, the MAC-D indicator crossed over negative, pointing to potential problems. In November, DOCU shares plunged in value.

This example illustrates that the MAC-D indicator used with a weekly chart can be a solid tool that can assist investors with avoiding over-priced stocks.

Percent Price Oscillator (PPO)

In 2019, Disney decided to extend its brand by getting into the highly competitive media streaming business. Stronger than expected competition combined with the onset of COVID which forced a shutdown of its theme parks, DIS shareholders started to lose faith in early 2021. Figure 9-4 illustrates weekly price action with the 40-week average overlaid and

Figure 9-3

DocuSign (DOCU) weekly chart with MAC-D indicator

Figure 9-4

Disney (DIS) weekly chart with MAC-D indicator

the Percent Price Oscillator (PPO) applied in the lower chart pane. In March 2021, the PPO crossed negative as DIS share price was testing the $200 level. This was an early warning sign for investors to perhaps think about exiting positions in Disney. In late October 2021, the PPO indicator breached the zero line as share price was in the $170 range. This was an even louder warning to exit. Since then, the PPO signaled a brief counter-trend rally in July 2022 which failed to penetrate the 40-week average. In January 2023, the PPO signaled another counter-trend rally; this one sparked by news that former CEO Bob Eiger was coming back to clean up the less and get the company on more solid footing again.

The PPO indicator used with a weekly chart can be a solid tool that can assist investors with decision making.

Fast Stochastic

As the US Federal Reserve piled liquidity into the financial system in 2020, bank stocks which had initially taken a severe beating began to recover. In November 2020, Citigroup (NYSE:C) began to rally from the low $40s. The Fast Stochastic crossing up and through its lower bound (20 level) was the first sign that a trend shift was underway. The Stochastic crossing above its upper bound (80 level) was another sign of the change. Share price ultimately rallied to test the $80 level. In June 2021, the Stochastic fell back beneath the upper bound. This was a sign to investors that the elevated share prices were going to soften. Share prices did in fact ease off, but did not fall beneath the 40-week average. By October 2021, the scenario was different. The Stochastic on two occasions had failed to get above its upper bound. And now price was breaking beneath the 40-week average as the Stochastic was crossing over negative. If there ever was a warning sign for investors to lighten up on share positions in Citigroup this was it. In January 2022, the Stochastic was emerging from beneath its lower bound and displaying a positive crossover. This price point was a Fibonacci 48.6% retracement of the November 2020 through June 2021

Figure 9-5

Citigroup (C) weekly chart with Fast Stochastic indicator

Figure 9-6

CF Industries (CF) weekly chart with Slow Stochastic indicator

rally. The counter-trend rally saw share price rise by nearly $10. The rally lost momentum as the Stochastic failed to rise above its upper bound. A similar counter-trend rally situation unfolded in July 2022 after price reached the 78.6% retracement level. The rally ran out of momentum, price turned lower and went on to retrace 100% of the November 2020 through June 2021 rally. At this time of writing, Citigroup share price is finally above its 40-week average again with the Stochastic confirming the trend has changed.

Slow Stochastic

CF Industries is the world's largest maker of granulated ammonia fertilizer. Figure 9-6 illustrates the weekly chart of CF Industries. The chart has been fitted with a 40-week average and the Slow Stochastic in the lower pane of the chart.

On a weekly chart basis, the Slow Stochastic can be interpreted using its upper and lower bounds (80 line and 20 line). As the Stochastic starts to rise above the lower bound, an investor with a longer time horizon would consider buying the shares. Ideally, such a move would also see price rise above its 40-week average. An investor would consider selling when the Stochastic breaks below the upper bound *and* when price breaks beneath its 40-week average.

In Figure 9-6, the September 2021 timeframe proved to be a buying opportunity. Price was getting support form the 40-week average and the Stochastic moved up and through its lower bound. Another similar buying opportunity made itself apparent in the August 2022 timeframe.

In December 2022, the Stochastic had already crossed beneath its upper bound. But now, price fell below the 40-week average. This was the exit sign for the offramp. At this time of writing in mid-February 2023, the Stochastic has just moved above its lower bound. What is needed now for investors to make a buying decision is for price to get above the $96 level and the 40-week average.

CHAPTER 10
CASE STUDIES

This final chapter contains a variety of charts analyzed for trend using the indicators and techniques discussed in the previous chapters. Studying these examples will solidify your understanding of the trend and how to delineate it. An exciting new way of looking at the markets with a new level of complexity awaits.

E-mini S&P 500 futures

At this time of writing in February 2023, the E-mini S&P 500 chart overlaid with a 200-day average tells the story: the major trend is bullish, the intermediate trend is bullish. From a swing low in October 2022, price moved higher into December before turning lower. The drawdown was a Fibonacci 61.8% retracement of the October-December leg higher. A buy signal materialized in January as price surpassed the prior swing high just above the 4000 level. However, the trend came under pressure as price neared the 78.6% retracement of the August-October decline. The 78.6% retracement set the stage for price to reverse its trend. The Fast Stochastic

Figure 10-1

E-mini S&P 500 (continuous front month contract) daily chart with Fast Stochastic

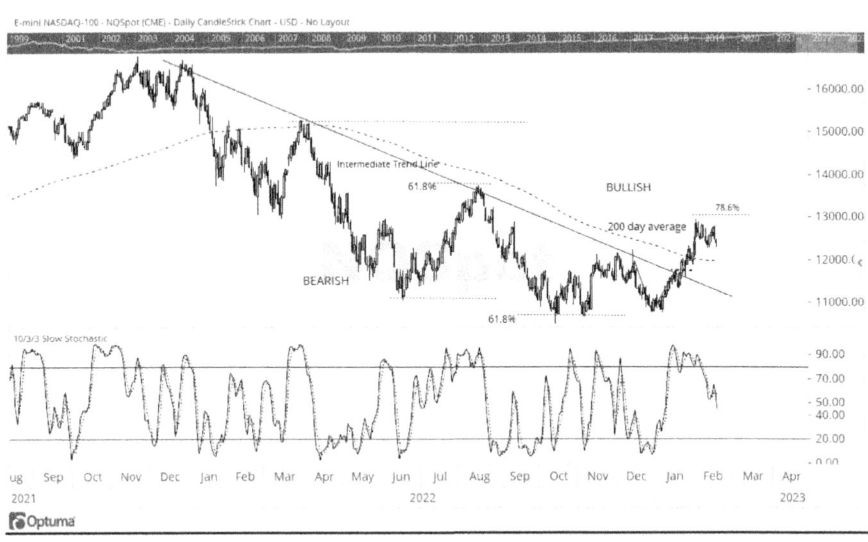

Figure 10-2

E-mini Nasdaq (continuous front month contract) daily chart with Fast Stochastic

indicator declined beneath its upper bound, confirming that trend had turned negative. At this time of writing, it was speculated that perhaps the S&P 500 would retrace to the 3950 level which would be a Fibonacci 61.8% retracement of the January-February leg higher. Although not shown in Figure 10-1, the situation proved far worse as a series of regional banks in the US failed, sending shivers through the market. Price would soon retrace 100% of its December to February gains.

E-mini Nasdaq futures

Tech stocks suffered mightily in 2022 as monetary conditions tightened and the stretched valuation multiples of the tech sector came under scrutiny. At this time of writing in February 2023, the Nasdaq chart shows a prevailing bullish major trend with price action trading above the 200-day average. The intermediate trend is also bullish.

From April 2022 through June 2022 the Nasdaq declined. The subsequent recovery from June through August was a Fibonacci 61.8% retracement. The Nasdaq then promptly rolled over with the Slow Stochastic falling beneath its upper bound line confirming the trend had changed. The decline continued into October 2022. The price level reached in October was a 61.8% retracement of the overall move from March 2020 through November 2021.

The Nasdaq then began a slow climb higher. By December, it has retraced 38.2% of the August-October decline. Unable to press higher, the Nasdaq rolled over and re-tested the October lows in late December.

As 2023 dawned, Nasdaq decided to stage another rally. In mid-January, the Slow Stochastic was indicating a buy signal; price was moving up and through the intermediate trend line, and a prior swing peak set-up was confirming the buy signal. Several days later, price moved up and through the 200-day average to create a bullish major trend. In early February, the Stochastic declined to beneath its upper bound suggesting a change in

Figure 10-3

WTI Crude (continuous front month contract) daily chart with Fast Stochastic

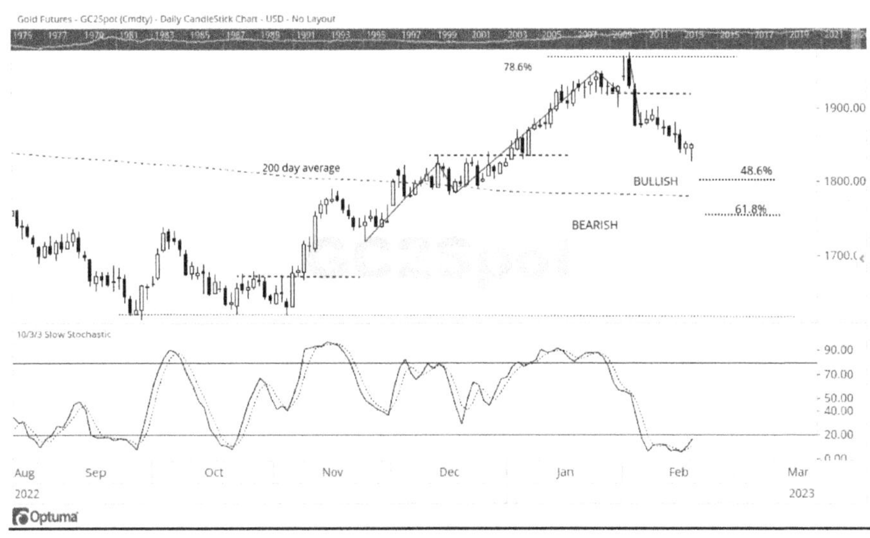

Figure 10-4

Gold (continuous front month contract) daily chart with Fast Stochastic

trend. This change came within 50 points of a full 78.6% retracement of the August-October decline.

A move to the 12,100 level would represent a Fibonacci 38.2% retracement of the December to February move up. A move to 11,600 would be a 61.8% retracement. In fact, what happened was a retracement of 48.6%.

WTI Crude Oil

Oil prices peaked in mid-2022 when the US government decided to tap into its Strategic Petroleum Reserves in an effort to halt the rising price of gasoline at the pumps. By late July, Oil price had broken beneath its 200-day average; the major trend was now bearish. An attempt at reversing this bearish situation was made in August, but to no avail. A pattern of lower price tops again established itself.

At this time of writing in February 2023, bearish major and intermediate trends continue to define the Oil market. A move above $80 per barrel will shift the intermediate trend to bullish. However, it will take a move to over $90 per barrel to see the major trend shift back to bullish.

The price lows made in December 2022 were a 38.2% retracement of the severe April 2020 lows to the March 2022 extreme peak. From the December low, Oil price moved higher into January 2023. This move was a Fibonacci 48.6% retracement of the decline from November through December 2022. This rally attempt stalled at the down-sloping intermediate trend line. A subsequent rally attempt in February also stalled at the intermediate trend line. The Slow Stochastic has now declined beneath its upper bound. The bearish trend on Oil seems to be entrenched.

Gold

Gold again visited the vaunted $2000 per ounce price point in April

Figure 10-5

Copper (continuous front month contract) daily chart with Fast Stochastic

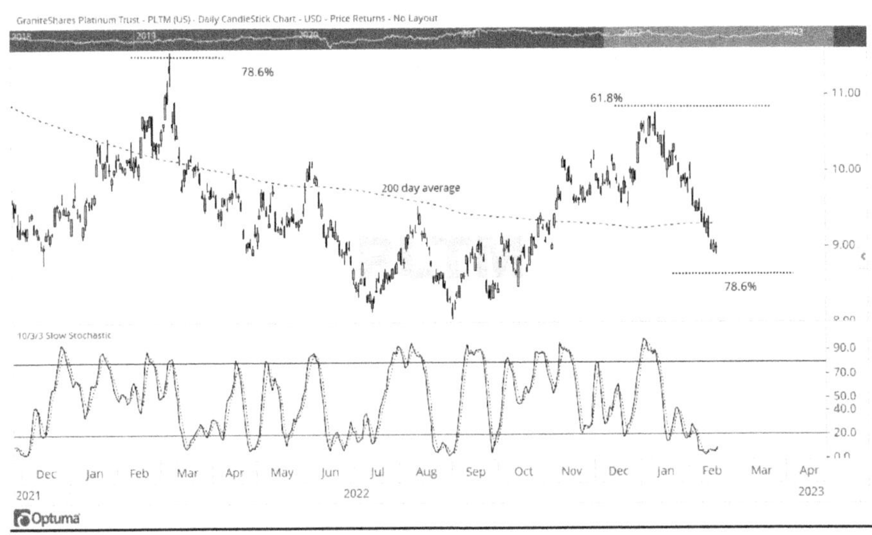

Figure 10-6

Platinum (PLTM ETF) daily chart with Fast Stochastic

2022. This was its third attempt at surpassing the $2000 level since 2011. Once again, Gold was unable to surpass this key psychological threshold. A bearish intermediate trend soon took form and a pattern of lower price peaks came into view. In June, Gold price slipped beneath the 200-day average, leading to a bearish major trend taking form.

Finally, in November 2022, as the US dollar reached a peak inflection point, Gold price started to orient itself higher. As price surpassed a prior peak, the Slow Stochastic offered confirmation of the changing trend. The down-trending intermediate trend line was quickly surpassed and the intermediate trend turned bullish. In December 2022, the 200-day average was surpassed to turn the major trend bullish. Price consolidated sideways into January 2023. As price moved above the consolidation channel, the Slow Stochastic moved above its upper bound line. Gold was acting as a hedge against the steady flow of negative news from the crypto currency sector, a hedge against uncertainty over the war in Ukraine, the possibility of recession, and the potential for relations with China to deteriorate further. In early February, Gold ran out of momentum at the $1975 level. The Gold bugs who were calling for a decisive move above $2000 per ounce were suddenly silenced. This price level was a Fibonacci 78.6% retracement of the March through November decline. As of February 2023, the major trend is still bullish, but a retracement is unfolding. A move to $1800 would be a 48.6% retracement and $1755 would be a 61.8% retracement.

Copper

Copper is essential to a global economy focused on vehicle electrification and green energy generation. This theme was largely forgotten about during the market ugliness that defined 2022. In late October 2022, investors found their bearings again and the Copper story came back into focus. By early November, Copper price was surpassing a prior high and surpassing the down-sloping intermediate trend line. The Slow Stochastic confirmed the trend change; a bullish intermediate trend was

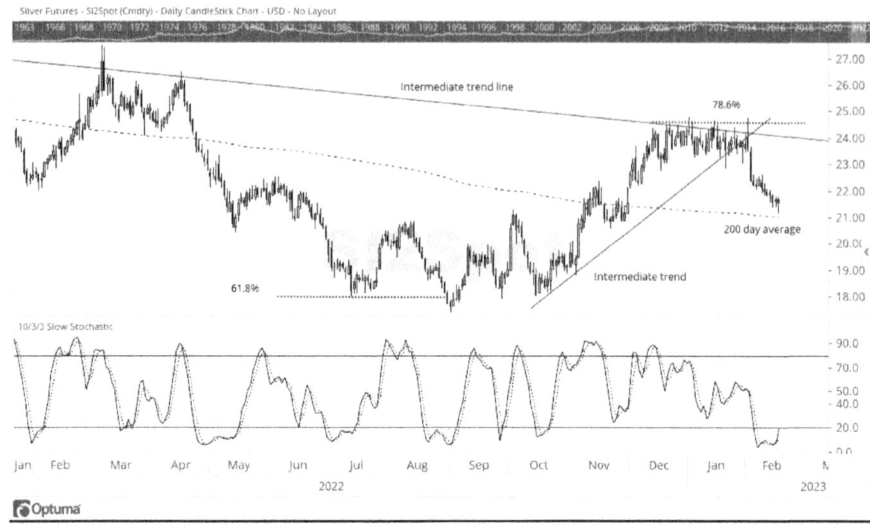

Figure 10-7

Silver (continuous front month contract) daily chart with Fast Stochastic

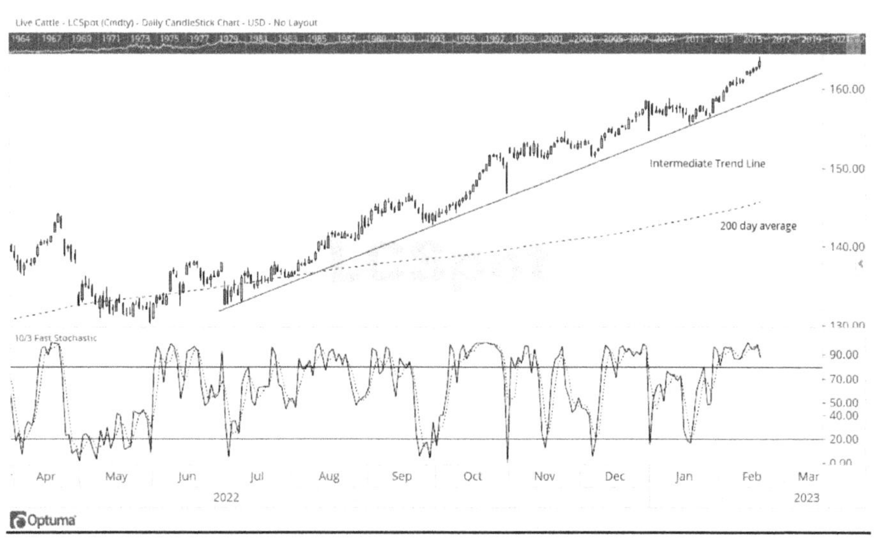

Figure 10-8

Live Cattle (continuous front month contract) daily chart with Fast Stochastic

now underway. In January 2023, price surpassed the 200-day average to usher in a bullish major trend.

The price high recorded in late January 2023 was an overlap of two Fibonacci retracements: a 61.8% retracement of the March to July 2022 decline, and a 78.6% retracement of the June-July 2022 leg down. At this time of writing, it is not surprising to see Copper prices consolidating sideways. The major and intermediate trends remain bullish. A move above the prior swing peak made in January 2023 will signal that Copper is staging its next advance.

Platinum

ETF Fund manager Granite Shares manages the PLTM product. This ETF is a physical inventory of Platinum metal held in a secure vault in London, U.K.

Between February 2021 and September 2022, Platinum metal prices declined. This was reflected in the declining price of this ETF. As Figure 10-6 shows, a counter-trend rally started in December 2021 and continued into February 2022. This rally retraced Fibonacci 61.8% of the down move from February – December 2021. This ETF briefly surpassed its 200-day average, setting the stage for a bullish major trend. But, the rally lost momentum at this key Fibonacci level. Price faded beneath the 200-day average and the falling Stochastic confirmed that the trend was resuming its negative tone. It would not be until September 2022 that Platinum metal prices would find a significant low, retesting its September 2020 lows. In hindsight, it could now be seen that the February 2022 rally peak had also been a 78.6% retracement of the overall February 2021 to September 2022 decline. Platinum prices then rallied into early 2023 running out of momentum just shy of the 61.8% retracement of the February 2021 to September 2022 decline. Price rolled over and at this time of writing, is headed for a 78.6% retracement of the September 2022 to January 2023 rally. The 200-day average has been breached. The

Figure 10-9

Soybeans (continuous front month contract) daily chart with Fast Stochastic

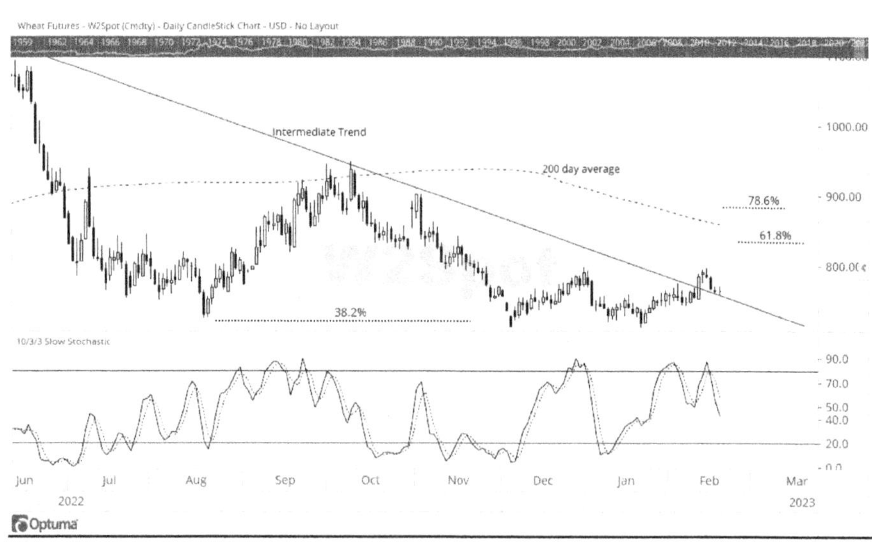

Figure 10-10

Wheat (continuous front month contract) daily chart with Fast Stochastic

Stochastic is deeply oversold and well beneath its lower bound. A test of the 78.6% retracement level followed by a favorable move by the Slow Stochastic will signal the start of a recovery and an advance higher on Platinum.

Silver

Silver prices began a slow, steady decline in early 2021. In April 2022, price broke the 200-day average, signaling the onset of a bearish major trend. By August 2022, Silver had found support at a Fibonacci 61.8% retracement of the March 2020-early 2021 advance.

After finding this floor of support, price began to move higher, surpassing the 200-day average in November 2022. However, by mid-December price was showing difficulty surpassing the 78.6% retracement of the April through August 2022 decline. In late January 2023, an up-sloping intermediate trend line was breached. At this time of writing, the 200-day average is under threat. A breach of this average will create a both a bearish intermediate and major trend.

A decline to the $25 per ounce level will signal a 61.8% retracement of the October through January move higher. A move to $19 per ounce will signal a full 78.6% retracement. A test of either of these levels will see the 200-day average broken. A subsequent move back above the 200-day average combined with the Stochastic moving above its upper bound will signal the start of a trend change.

Live Cattle

As the price of beef at your local supermarket suggests, the price trend on Live Cattle is bullish. This has generally been so since 2020. From 2014 through early 2020, Live Cattle prices steadily moved lower, prompting many ranchers to exit the cattle business. These exits created a supply chain shortage of beef. As of March 2023, this is reflected in the fast-food

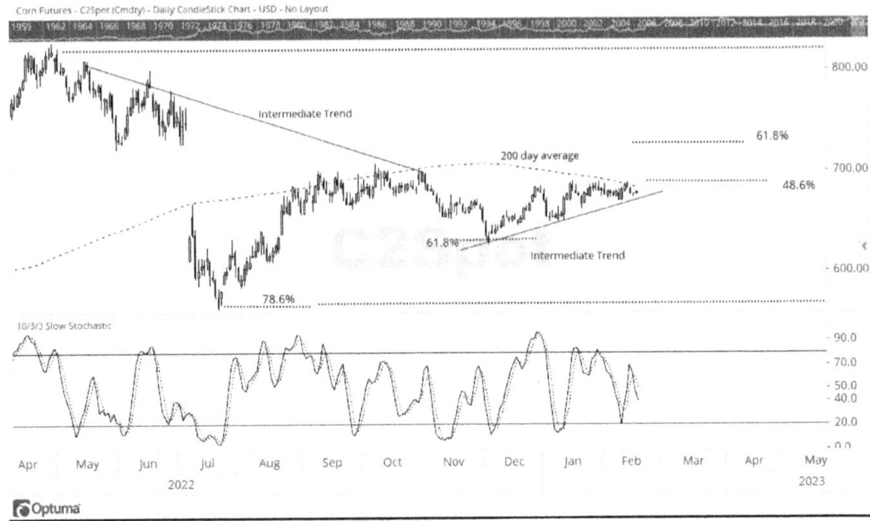

Figure 10-11

Corn (continuous front month contract) daily chart with Fast Stochastic

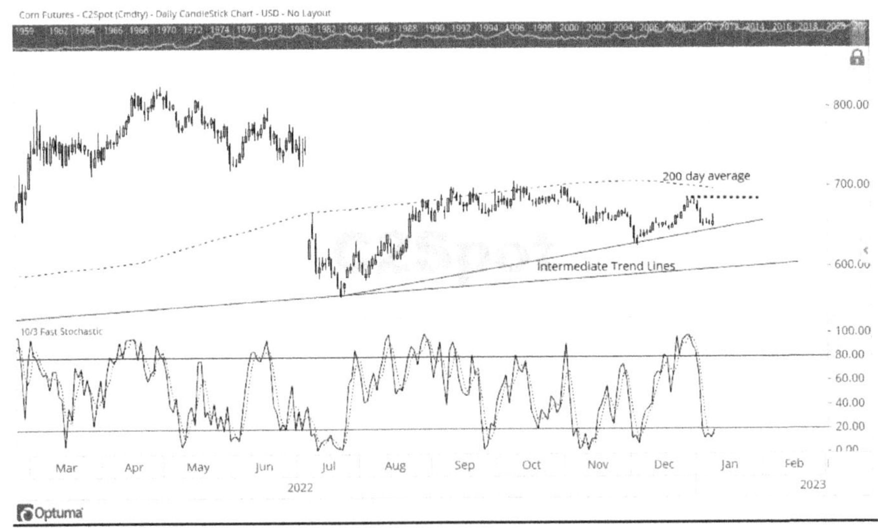

Figure 10-12

Cameco (TSX:CCO) daily chart with Fast Stochastic

industry with McDonalds' marketing of its new product, the 'Chicken Big Mac.'

As Figure 10-8 illustrates, both the major and intermediate trends remain bullish as of late February 2023. Price has surpassed a full Fibonacci 78.6% retracement of the 2014 to 2020 decline. This implies that a re-test of the 2014 highs at the $171 level is in order. With trends being bullish, a trader could have bought futures on any dips after getting confirmation from an indicator such as the Fast Stochastic.

Soybeans

Soybeans at this time of writing are in a bullish intermediate trend. Price is close to surpassing the 200-day average to signal a bullish major trend. The current rally started on October 2022 after Soybean prices had retraced 61.8% of the move from late 2021 through June 2022.

If price can surpass $15.50 per bushel, that will be a Fibonacci 48.6% retracement of the June through October 2022 decline. The Slow Stochastic recently failed to penetrate its upper bound. The Stochastic moving above its upper bound combined with Soybeans moving above the 48.6% retracement level will set the stage for a test of the 61.8% retracement level at the $16.20 per bushel level.

Wheat

Wheat prices experienced some wild price excursions earlier in 2022; would Ukrainian wheat exports be allowed to leave the country, or not?

As deals were reached to allow Ukrainian wheat to exit the country, the price of Chicago Wheat futures faded to a low in August 2022. The support level found in August was a Fibonacci 38.2% of the overall 2016 through 2022 price advance.

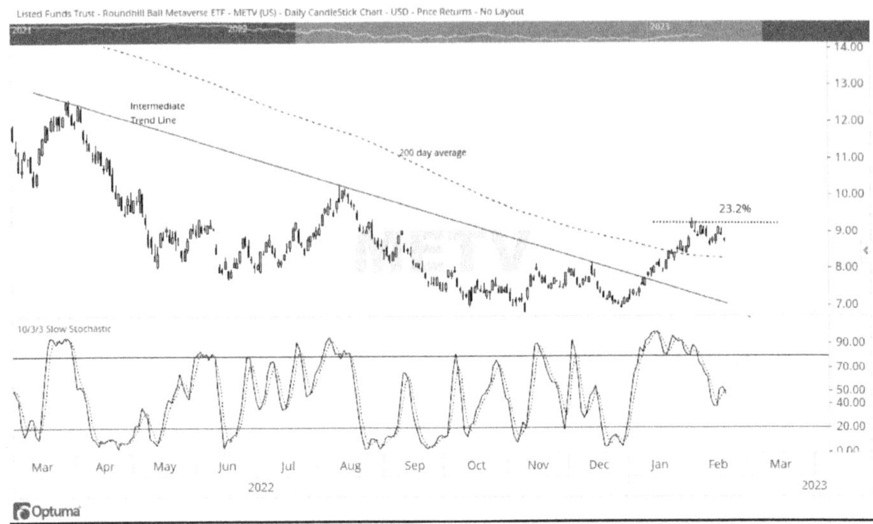

Figure 10-13

Roundhill Investments Metaverse ETF (METV) daily chart with Fast Stochastic

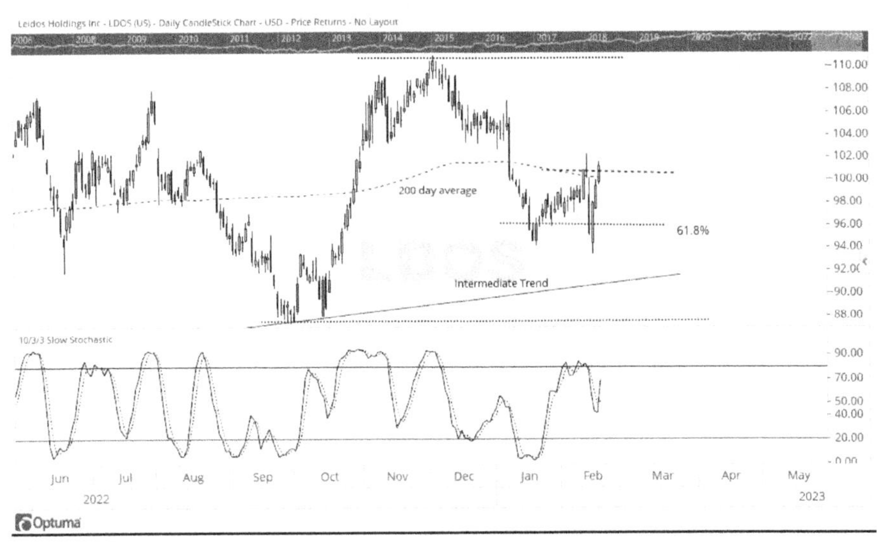

Figure 10-14

Leidos Holdings (LDOS) daily chart with Fast Stochastic

From the August low, a rally failed to penetrate the 200-day average and swing the major trend bullish. A retest of the August support level then followed in December.

As of this time of writing in February 2023, the major trend remains bearish. Price is struggling to get above the down-sloping intermediate trend line. The Stochastic is beneath its upper bound, confirming the price weakness.

If geopolitical pressures impact the Spring seeding efforts in Ukraine, Chicago Wheat might well stage a rally. A move to the $8.35 per bushel level would be a 61.8% retracement of the October-December 2022 decline. A 78.6% retracement of this decline would put prices above the 200-day average and set the stage for a bullish major trend.

Corn

Corn, much like Wheat, experienced some wild price volatility earlier in 2022; would Ukrainian corn exports be allowed to leave the country, or not? In the end, deals were struck. Corn was allowed to be exported. Chicago Corn futures fell in price, finding a floor of support in July 2022. The support level was a 38.2% retracement of the August 2020 to April 2022 advance. This level was also a 61.8% retracement of the October 2021 to April 2022 advance. This level was also a 38.2% retracement of the move from August 2020 to April 2022.

The major trend on Corn is bearish as of this time of writing in February 2023. However, the encouraging news is the intermediate trend has a bullish tone to it. A move above $6.85 per bushel will see price surpass a swing peak made in late December 2022 and record a 48.6% retracement of the April-July 2022 lower. Moreover, the 200-day average will be surpassed and a bullish major trend will take shape.

The Stochastic is suggesting that such a move does not have the potential

Figure 10-15

BitCoin futures (continuous front month) daily chart with KST Indicator

at this moment. Should the Stochastic start to suggest otherwise, and if geopolitical tensions re-assert themselves, Corn prices could quickly move up to test the 61.8% retracement level at $7.25 per bushel.

Uranium

Uranium as a fuel source for generating power received a black eye in 2011 with the nuclear reactor disaster in Fukushima, Japan.

There is an intriguing story developing behind the scenes with regards to the future of nuclear. In the 1950s, researchers at the Oak Ridge Laboratories in Tennessee embarked on two divergent paths. One path involved a nuclear reactor based on molten salt technology. The other focused on a reactor design with a water-based reactor core. The water based design won the day and the salt-based technology was shelved. Several years ago, NASA revived the molten salt design concept to address the question of what type of reactor could be placed on the Moon to act as a power source. Fast forward to today and Bill Gates is behind a private company that has made leaps and bounds to advance the safer, molten salt design. Nuclear will be part of our vocabulary once again.

Canadian Uranium miner Cameco is a good proxy for the nuclear story, especially with their recent joint venture purchase of nuclear power plant manufacturer Westinghouse. Cameco as of mid-January 2023 was enjoying bullish intermediate and major trends. The volatility of the share price makes Cameco something that traders can follow. The Fast Stochastic and the price/prior swing strategy will be two excellent tools to use in 2023 and beyond.

Metaverse

Another theme that will endure beyond 2023 is the Metaverse. Roundhill Investments has assembled an ETF that it feels represents the key players that will be advancing the metaverse theme. While these tech companies are under pressure thanks to the market performance in 2022, as the Metaverse theme evolves and takes shape, this ETF might be a good way to take advantage. The Fast Stochastic will help you in your trading efforts. As of this time of writing, METV is showing a bullish intermediate trend and a bullish major trend. The price history of this ETF is limited. However, at this time of writing, price has retraced Fibonacci 23.2% of the 2022 decline.

Artificial Intelligence

Another theme that will gain in popularity going forward is artificial intelligence. There was a time when companies would hire quality control engineers to gather process data. The data would be parsed and analyzed in the context of a quality assurance program. Fast forward to the present and today the gathering and parsing of data is done by computer-driven sensors. The data is fed into algorithms that look for patterns. Breaches of these patterns trigger human intervention to resolve the problems. One company that is a leader in the AI field is Leidos Holdings (LDOS).

Leidos share price swings back and forth above and below its 200-day average. Leidos is a moneymaker; no question about it. However, its major customer is the US government. As government spending remains under scrutiny, LDOS remains uncertain as to the portion of its overall revenue that will come from government. The share price volatility makes it a good trading candidate. Price surpassing prior swing peaks are valuable events to be alert to. The Slow Stochastic is a powerful ally to use as well. At this time of writing, a move higher that takes out the recent February swing peak will be a buy signal. Near term support is at the 61.8% retracement of the October-December 2022 advance.

Crypto / BitCoin

I will conclude this chapter with a look at the cryptocurrency phenomenon. At this time of writing, the dark side of crypto is on full display as the FTX

/ Sam Bankman Fried drama plays out. Other names in the fray include Barry Silbert (Genesis crypto exchange), the Winklevoss twins (Gemini crypto exchange), and Changpeng Zhao (Binance crypto exchange). In my opinion, the negative news shall pass. Crypto is not going away. The transition from unregulated, wild-west action to a more sane, more regulated landscape is a work in progress.

The first quarter of 2023 has been full of drama in the crypto currency space. One would think that BitCoin would have probed the single digit price levels, but, not so. It appears that BitCoin might be finding support in the $24,000 neighborhood. I am not advising that readers of this book rush out and buy, but the fact that BitCoin is still holding its value says to me that the crypto story will be around for a while yet. Figure 10-15, fitted with the KST indicator, shows that the major trend is bullish, by a slim margin. The intermediate trend is likewise bullish, but again by a slender margin. A Fibonacci 23.2% retracement of the November 2021 to December 2022 move will occur at the $28,000 per coin level. A move still higher will see the 38.2% retracement level of $36,000 come into focus.

FINAL WORD

This book has taken you on an intense journey into technical chart indicators. Some of these indicators trace their origins to the 1950s when Ralph Dystant and his dedicated team of traders in Chicago spent hours each day updating charts with nothing more than an adding machine, paper, and a pencil. The late 1970s saw a few further refinements to chart indicators thanks to traders like Gerald Appel and J. Welles Wilder. With the advent of personal computers in the late 1980s, came a literal avalanche of chart indicators. Gone were the adding machines, paper, and pencils. Now open, high, low, and close price data could be typed into a computer program. Algorithms were created to massage this data and generate copious numbers of indicators. Fast forward to today and the number of indicators that come pre-programmed into a typical market software program is staggering.

Years ago, when I was studying for my CFA credential, I hit a mental roadblock when the curriculum material very strongly suggested that technical chart analysis did not work. I have not forgotten that stinging criticism. Ever the obstinate contrarian, I have since made it a point to more deeply explore various chart indicators and the mathematics that underpin them.

In 2022, while coaching clients on how to incorporate astrology into their stock market buying and selling activity, it became apparent to me that there was a general lack of knowledge of chart indicators and how to use them. I decided to write a book that would serve as a convenient desktop reference for traders and investors. I hope that this publication stimulates you to start using technical chart indicators in your market activity. I hope you enjoy using this book as much as I have enjoyed writing it.

ABOUT THE AUTHOR

Malcolm Bucholtz, B.Sc., MBA, M.Sc., is a graduate of Queen's University (Faculty of Engineering) in Canada and Heriot Watt University in Scotland (where he received an MBA degree and a M.Sc. degree). After working in Canadian industry for far too many years, Malcolm followed his passion for the financial markets by becoming an Investment Advisor/Commodity Trading Advisor with an independent brokerage firm in western Canada. Today, he resides in a small town in southern Saskatchewan, Canada where he trades the financial markets using technical chart analysis, esoteric mathematics, and the planetary/cosmic principles outlined in his various other books.

His first book, **The Bull, the Bear, and the Planets**, offers the reader an introduction to financial astrology and makes the case that there are esoteric and astrological phenomena that influence the financial markets. His second book, **The Lost Science**, takes the reader on a deeper journey into planetary events and unique mathematical phenomena that influence financial markets. His third book, **De-Mystifying the McWhirter**

Theory of Stock Market Forecasting, seeks to simplify and illustrate the McWhirter methodology. The ***Cosmic Clock*** follows from the ***Lost Science*** and helps the reader become better acquainted with planetary events that influence markets. Malcolm has been writing the ***Financial Astrology Almanac*** each year since 2014.

Malcolm maintains a website (**www.investingsuccess.ca**) where he provides traders and investors with astrological insights into the financial markets. He also offers the *Astrology Letter* service where subscribers receive twice-monthly previews of pending astrological events that stand to influence markets. He also offers the *Cycle Report* where subscribers are kept apprised on cyclical turning points based on Hurst cycles.

OTHER BOOKS BY THE AUTHOR

The Bull, The Bear and The Planets

Once maligned by many, the subject of financial astrology is now experiencing a revival as traders and investors seek deeper insight into the forces that move the financial markets.

The markets are a dynamic entity fueled by many factors, some of which we can easily comprehend, some of which are esoteric. *The Bull, The Bear and the Planets* introduces the reader to the notion that astrological phenomena can influence price action on financial markets and create trend changes across both short and longer term time horizons. From an introduction to the historical basics behind astrology through to an examination of lunar astrology and planetary aspects, the numerous illustrated examples in this book will introduce the reader to the power of astrology and its impact on both equity markets and commodity futures markets.

The Lost Science

The financial markets are a reflection of the psychological emotions of traders and investors. These emotions ebb and flow in harmony with the forces of nature.

Scientific techniques and phenomena such as square root mathematics, the Golden Mean, the Golden Sequence, lunar events, planetary transits and planetary aspects have been used by civilizations dating as far back as the ancient Egyptians in order to comprehend the forces of nature.

The emotions of traders and investors can fluctuate in accordance with these forces of nature. Lunar events can be seen to align with trend changes on financial markets. Significant market cycles align with planetary transits and aspects. Price patterns on stocks, commodity futures and market indices can be seen to conform to square root and Golden Mean mathematics.

In the early years of the 20th century the most successful traders on Wall Street, including the venerable W.D. Gann, used these scientific techniques and phenomena to profit from the markets. However, over the ensuing decades as technology has advanced, the science has been lost.

The Lost Science acquaints the reader with an extensive range of astrological and mathematical phenomena. From the Golden Mean and Fibonacci Sequence, to planetary transit lines and square roots through to an examination of lunar and planetary aspects, the numerous illustrated examples in this book show the reader how these unique scientific phenomena impact the financial markets.

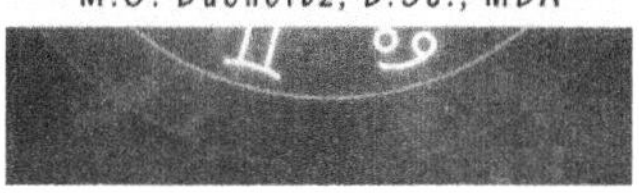

Stock Market Forecasting –
The McWhirter Method
De-Mystified

M.G. Bucholtz, B.Sc., MBA

Stock Market Forecasting: The McWhirter Method De-Mystified

Very little is known about Louise McWhirter, except that in 1937 she wrote the book, *McWhirter Theory of Stock Market Forecasting.*

In my travels to places as far away as the British Library in London, England to research financial Astrology, not once did I come across any other books written by McWhirter. Not once did I find any other book from her era that even mentioned her name. I find all of this to be deeply mysterious. Whoever she was, she wrote only one book. It is a powerful one that is as accurate today as it was back in 1937. The purpose of writing this book is suggested by the title itself – to de-mystify McWhirter's methodology.

The Cosmic Clock

Can the movements of the Moon affect the stock market?

Are price swings on Crude Oil, Soybeans, the British pound and other financial instruments a reflection of planetary placements?

The answer to these questions is YES. Changes in price trends on the markets are in fact related to our changing emotions.

Our emotions, in turn, are impacted by the changing events in our cosmos.

In the early part of the 20th century, many successful traders on Wall Street, including the venerable W.D. Gann and the mysterious Louise McWhirter, understood that emotion was linked to the forces of the cosmos. They used astrological events and esoteric mathematics to predict changes in price trend and to profit from the markets.

However, by the latter part of the 20th century, the investment community had become more comfortable in relying on academic financial theory and the opinions of colorful television media personalities, all wrapped up in a buy and hold mentality.

The Cosmic Clock has been written for traders and investors who are seeking to gain an understanding of the cosmic forces that influence emotion and the financial markets.

This book will acquaint you with an extensive range of astrological and mathematical phenomena—from the Golden Mean and Fibonacci Sequence through planetary transit lines, quantum lines, the McWhirter method, planetary conjunctions and market cycles. The numerous illustrated examples show how these unique phenomena can deepen your understanding of the financial markets with the goal of making you a better trader and investor.

Made in the USA
Las Vegas, NV
01 May 2023

71386176R00109